Becoming Who God Intended

"Isolates the issues people have and gives solutions in a way that's fresh and profoundly biblical."

—Josh McDowell

"David Eckman is a man you can trust...His teaching resonates with God's wisdom and compassion."

—Stu Weber, author of
Tender Warrior and *Four Pillars of a Man's Heart*

"Dr. Eckman's wisdom and vision helped me come face-to-face with issues I thought I had addressed long ago...The pain I have lived with so long is now gone, thanks to being able to give all of my family background over to God."

—Cheryl, Sacramento, California

"In reaching our students in the areas of their heart...in dealing with areas of addictions, eating disorders, and sexual disorders, nothing we've done has been more effective than what Dr. Eckman and his team have done for us."

—Tim Rule, Northwest Associate Director,
Campus Crusade for Christ

"Thank you, Dr. Eckman, for visiting our women's group and presenting a talk about how our Daddy Father sees us...I love my family history as viewed by my Abba...and it makes me even like myself!"

—Yemi, San Jose, California

"God has given David powerful insights to help people discover who they are in Christ and show them what a huge difference this truth can make in everyday life."

—Chip Ingram, President, Walk Thru the Bible Ministries;
author of *The Invisible War*

"I enjoyed reading *Becoming Who God Intended* and found it both encouraging and helpful to me personally...I especially like what Dr. Eckman writes about the imagination. I'm a big believer in submitting our imaginations to the Holy Spirit in order to allow Him to 'reprogram our minds' about who our Abba-Father really is."

—Steve McVey, author of *Grace Walk*

Sex
Food
&God

David Eckman

HARVEST HOUSE PUBLISHERS

EUGENE, OREGON

All Scripture quotations are the author's own translations. Any emphases or bracketed interpolations have been inserted by the author.

Cover by Koechel Peterson & Associates, Inc., Minneapolis, Minnesota

Cover photos © Photos.com

SEX, FOOD, AND GOD
Copyright © 2006 by David Eckman
Published by Harvest House Publishers
Eugene, Oregon 97402
www.harvesthousepublishers.com

Library of Congress Cataloging-in-Publication Data

Eckman, David, 1947-
  Sex, food, and God / David Eckman.
     p. cm.

  ISBN-13: 978-0-7369-1785-8
  ISBN-10: 0-7369-1785-3
  1. Habit breaking—Religious aspects—Christianity. 2. Compulsive behavior—Religious aspects—Christianity. 3. Sex addiction—Religious aspects—Christianity. 4. Compulsive eating—Religious aspects—Christianity. 5. Temptation. 6. Sin. I. Title.
  BV4598.7.E25 2006
  241'.68—dc22

                                                            2006013544

Printed in the United States of America

         06 07 08 09 10 11 12 13 14 / VP-SK / 10 9 8 7 6 5 4 3 2 1

*To those who shared their
pilgrimage with me in the
writing of this book*

and

*To the greatest pilgrim of them all,
my wife, Carol*

Acknowledgments

I must thank Tammy Jo Wickersheim for sharing her story as a living illustration of the principles of this book. Also, Jennifer Chui, Doctor of Pharmacy, has been very helpful in sharing insights from her area of expertise.

Contents

The World of Walking Backward

In the World of Walking Backward, men and women walk backward wherever they go. It's amazing to go to stores and shopping centers and watch hundreds of people walking through the aisles, down the stairs, up the escalators—all backward.

Everyone who lives in the World of Walking Backward has overdeveloped neck muscles. It's pretty extraordinary how well people can twist their heads around and look at all of life backward.

When children are being raised in the World of Walking Backward, they are taught to walk backward. A stubborn few try to walk forward, but that is soon spanked out of them. When really deep thinkers bring up the idea that walking backward is unnatural, they are scorned as impractical, otherworldly types with overactive imaginations—even rebels or anarchists. But since everyone in the World of Walking Backward walks backward, the social pressure to walk that way is so immense that sooner or later everyone succumbs.

The world of temptation, compulsion, and addiction is just as uncomfortable, troublesome, and accident-prone as the backward world I describe above. But those who are caught up in addictive behaviors find it just as hard to believe that there is a much easier, more natural way to live. Just as people are meant to be happy and content walking forward, so are people meant to live happily and successfully without mismanaged sexuality and eating.

Addiction is always the backward use of what God intended to be much easier and happier. Addiction is the misuse of the good. What this book offers is the way to step out of temptation, compulsion, and addiction…and step into the world of using what is within us for our good, especially food and sex. Leaving addiction behind will bring a person into a world that eventually will feel good and complete and happy. What this book is about is how to enter that world and stay there.

≈

You do not have to be addicted to benefit from the contents of this book. You just have to be like the rest of us—surprised by how compelling food and sexuality can be, and surprised by how weak-willed we appear to be. As I survey some of the concepts we're going to cover, you may also find one, several, or all of them to be surprising to you—and perhaps of special interest or help.

What You'll Find in the Following Chapters

Gifts, addictions, and God. Perhaps you want to learn how to make the best use of the good gifts of life, like food and sexuality. Or perhaps you want to see how the good things of life relate to God. On the other side, maybe you want to discover why temptation, compulsion, and addiction are so powerful in our lives. In all these cases, this book is for you.

An example of a journey to freedom. If you want to see what God can do with a life trapped by different forms of addiction, later in this book you will read the story of Tammy Jo. She was codependent—she panicked without a man in her life. She was addicted to tobacco. And she was anorexic. She had every reason in the world to be stuck in addictions. Born out of wedlock, sexually abused from the age of five, a victim of the pornography trade, married at age 14, bereaved of a beloved daughter…her heartaches seem endless. We will see how she was brought out of that.

Ways to deal with a trap you're in. If you are caught up in an addiction, this book is for you. As a prime example, pornography and sexual temptation and addiction are now serious issues not for just men but also women, and so a fresh look is needed to deal with that onslaught. Increasing numbers of women are trapped by the crack cocaine of Internet porn, as shown by the fact that 32 million American women had visited at least one pornography Web site in one month of 2004 alone. And 25 million Americans visit cybersex sites for between one and ten hours per week, with another 4.7 million doing so in excess of eleven hours per week.*

The relationship of family background to temptation, compulsion, and addiction. If you think there is a connection between family background and adult addiction, again, this book is for you. To underscore the Bible's approach on this issue, we will draw information from the largest study done on the subject in the history of the world. The *Adverse Childhood Experiences Study* was carried out by the CDC (Centers for Disease Control) and Kaiser Permanente (the largest HMO in the country) to examine the connection between bad experiences in childhood and adult health. The results are stunning…and may make you look at all of life in a different way.

The connection between pain—especially emotional pain and stress—and temptation, compulsion, and addiction. Just to give you a quick look at what is coming later, consider an amazing statistic found in medical literature. Heroin use was common among American soldiers fighting in Vietnam. Many of them would simply have

---

* Pamela Paul, *Pornified: How Pornography is Transforming Our Lives, Our Relationships, and Our Families* (New York: Henry Holt and Company, 2005); MSNBC/Stanford/Duquesne Study; Associated Press Online, 2/29/2000. The genders differ markedly in how they approach Internet pornography: Men visit online visual porn twice as much as women, and women favor chat rooms twice as much as men. Women, however, are more likely to sexually act out their chat-room relationships than men and carry them into the outside world. What we have seen on college campuses is that women, more and more, are approaching sexuality as men have. They are as flagrant, aggressive, and open to pornography as men.

been considered hopeless addicts. Yet within ten months after such soldiers returned to the United States, only 5 percent were still injecting heroin. There is no program in the world that has had such medically incredible success. Alcoholics Anonymous looks feeble in comparison. What brought about such an unbelievable cure rate?

In dealing with addiction, the assumption is almost universal that it is the chemicals that get a person hooked, and the chemicals that keep them hooked. That idea is utterly contradicted by the results of the "no-bullets-flying therapy" (in other words, getting out of Vietnam and away from the immense, moment-by-moment anxiety and danger)—which brought about a 95-percent cure rate among "participants." This leads to a truth we will spend several chapters exploring: *Reduce the heart's pain, and addiction drifts away.*

If you want to know why this principle is not only true, but profoundly biblical and vastly effective, this book is for you. And we will answer two questions:

1. What is the most effective way to reduce the pain within?

2. How do we use a pain-free heart to address the challenge of temptation, compulsion, and addiction?

The possibility of "addiction-proofing." If the principle we just mentioned is true—reduce the pain, emotional or physical, and addiction drifts away—there is one more implication: *Making our hearts and lives "addiction-proof" becomes a real possibility.*

Whether it is food addiction, heroin addiction, sex addiction, alcohol addiction, workaholism, rageaholism, or any of the other two dozen or so compulsions/addictions, we will learn how to protect our hearts from being enslaved. As we grasp truths about addiction and pain in the heart, our hearts can then relax and thrive under God's kindness and grace. In other words, we can start to develop a romance with God, which is the best (and really, the only) method of true *addiction-proofing.*

To pull together into one phrase what I've been saying, *the goal of this book is to show you how to have a happy heart.* Now, you might react to that statement in one of two ways:

- "A 'happy heart'? Dr. Eckman, that phrase sounds goofy, like 'they all lived happily ever after.' Isn't unhappiness the deepest reality of human existence? Life on earth is crappy, and I think you're living in a fantasy world."

- "Dr. Eckman, I feel pretty happy and content most of the time. Aren't people who are unhappy—and then get into addictions and so on—choosing to be that way? I think they'd feel better if they just made better choices."

To the group responding the first way, I want to mention my own background. I grew up in an alcoholic home—that is, in the World of Walking Backward. During my nearly 20 years in that world I did not believe there was such a thing as happiness. But the truth is, *that* is the fantasy world.

Today I know different, and I believe that a vibrant Christian spirituality is the way to eventually feel good and complete and happy. What do you have to lose? You will probably not be *un*happier after reading this book…and you might find contentment and joy you can't conceive of right now.

To the people responding the second way, I would say that it is crucial for you to understand the mental/emotional world the other half lives in (I sometimes call it the "opposite world"). You have to deal with such people all the time. Many of them may end up among (or now be among) your family and friends. Do you want to connect—deeply connect—with people you know and love? Do you want to protect their hearts from addiction, compulsion, and temptation, even though these things are not such a struggle for you? And do you want to be prepared in case *you* get blindsided by an overpowering urge that could pull you down into misery?

In either case, this book really is for you. I invite you to turn the page and learn more.

PART ONE

Understanding Appetites, Addiction, and Anesthesia

ONE

Gift Abuse

We have talked about the World of Walking Backward and its discomforts, and how it is very similar to the world of temptation and addiction. In that world, sex, food, and other things are used in a thoroughly backward way, and that goes unnoticed. In fact, addictive behaviors seem natural to those captured by them.

Abusing the Pleasures of Life

Everything involved in addiction is good. If it is food addiction—some variety of binging, purging, anorexia, or overeating—just attend a weight-reduction class and you will discover how good food really is. (And you'll be able to get some of the best recipes around.) I can remember attending one such class where the entire time was given over to low-calorie recipes. The woman instructor was going over in detail how to lose weight through eating differently, and she shared a lot of low-calorie desserts. After each recipe there was an "ooh and aah" of appreciation from the women present. Being the lone man, I watched and listened with fascination. Obviously the women who were there were very enthusiastic about what they were struggling to manage. They thought food was great!

In a group of men or women who are struggling with sexual addiction you would not find them sharing how much they really enjoyed sex (unlike overeaters). But everyone there would assume sexuality is pleasurable—and a good and great thing to have if managed properly. The problem is the misuse of a good thing.

> Addiction to swallowing glass does not exist. Instead, temptation, compulsion, and addiction involve good things.

Julie uses shopping to get her mind off an uncomfortable marriage. She dreads the credit-card bill at the end of the month because it is the only time she has a sense of the problem she is struggling with. Yet if we looked at every item on the bill, it would be something good for someone. Whether a new outfit for her infant or a new chair for the living room, she could explain the value of each item. Further, she spent a lot of time and care in getting just the right thing. Thought, care, and comforts are not bad, but too much preoccupation and too many expenditures lead to financial disaster. If we walked through Julie's home, however, we would enjoy all the good things we see.

José is an exercise buff. He works as an army recruiter, and in his job he is expected to look trim and muscular. What you would not know is that every evening after work he is at the gym and not home. Megan, his wife, feels abandoned and is losing patience with his explanations about how important exercise is. He does not know it, but he is heading for a divorce. But when he signs the divorce papers, he will look great! Exercise is great too. People who exercise look trim. More than that, the doctors think it's good to do. But when a person is exercising so much that key people in their lives are ignored, a good thing is being misused.

Addiction to swallowing glass does not exist. Instead, temptation, compulsion, and addiction involve good things. So the challenge is to enjoy what comes into our lives and not become mastered by them.

Why is this important to you? Because people who are struggling with food or sex find their inner life a place of discomfort and often confusion. The intention of this book is to show you how to truly enjoy what is inside including the appetites. As you read you will see that everything about you is meant for your good and God's glory. The real issue is how to turn our inner life from a place of discomfort to a healed place of enjoyment, and not slavery.

What's Good About Alcohol and Heroin?

"I can see that sex and food are good things misused," some might say, "but what about heroin and other drugs? They are certainly not good things being misused!"

We have to follow two steps to see how substances misuse the blessings of life. God has given us a good set of chemicals that are designed to bring us pleasure as we are in positive relationships. When we are in family relationships and are sensing attachment, the chemicals oxytocin and vasopressin are present. When we are having fun and romance, dopamine and serotonin are present. When we are sexually involved in a healthy way, testosterone is present. Those chemicals are present throughout healthy relationships. Truly we can't help but believe that they are good things!

But we can get those good things other ways too. Oxytocin and vasopressin likely can be produced by self-absorbed narcissism. Certainly substance abuse (alcohol, drugs) and gambling can produce rivers of dopamine and serotonin. Methamphetamines—meth— also produces serotonin, dopamine, and epinephrine. Pornography and sexual addiction can produce testosterone.

The goal of substance abuse is to produce—and overproduce— the chemicals that flow out of good relationships. *Substance abuse is an end run around relationships: The sensation is everything.* What alcoholism and drug abuse do is manufacture chemicals that are recognizably good. Heroin and drugs are not good things, but they produce the chemicals that were designed to enhance and sustain healthy relationships!

The deeper reality is, our very body chemistry, another good but hidden gift from God, can be misused by drugs and alcohol to circumvent the relationships and achievements that would very naturally produce them in healthy amounts.

As an example, on the Internet there is a Web site that talks about oxytocin; it is called the love drug. We no longer need God because all we have to do is inject oxytocin. The author of the article is dead serious. He maintains that belief in God produces oxytocin, the chemical of secure and caring relationships. So forget God—just get the chemical.

If we follow his logic, we would have the plot from the movie *The Matrix.* There people were submerged in a chemical bath, connected to tubes and electrodes, and their mind was experiencing a virtual world through electronic means. Good positive chemicals are the results of God and relationships with people, but the movie simplified everything and got rid of relationships with people and just substituted chemicals. Or the same result can be gotten in a more everyday way. Instead of spouses and children, let us have a carton of daily pills that can make us feel good without any messy people involved! But Christianity intends that we should feel good and have relationships with God and people at the same time.

So everything involved with temptation, compulsion, and addiction is a good thing. The challenge this book will take up is to show how healthy management of good things stops addiction in its tracks.

Understanding the Source of the Good Gifts

All of the realities involved with addiction are good because a good-hearted God made them that way. That's important because it means originally everything within us was designed to bring us deep satisfaction and joy. If that is so—and it is—it means we can really be hopeful that managing ourselves and having joy is entirely possible.

In the Genesis account of the creation of the earth and Adam and Eve, the constantly repeated reality is that creation is good.

> God proceeded to say, "Let there be light, and there came to be light. And God saw that the light was good" (Genesis 1:3-4).*

The Hebrew word for good is *tov;* it refers to something being beneficial. Without light, life would not be, and reality for us would not be seen. It is an understatement to say light is beneficial!

The word *beneficial* is repeated seven times in the chapter for what goes on in each creative day. The refrain from God is that everything He created is good, or beneficial. Notice that it is describing the creations of the six days and the word good is repeated seven times. On the sixth day when animals and humanity (male and female) are created, God said that the beasts, the animals, and the creepy-crawlies all are good or beneficial, as is humanity. Then, a segment occurs wherein two members of the Trinity (almost certainly the Father and the Son) have a conversation. No divine dialogue occurred concerning the light, the waters, the land mass (the earth), the birds, the fish, the stars, the sun and moon, or the animals. But after the divine conversation a man and a woman were made. At that point, God looked over the whole of His creative work, with humanity at the pinnacle, and he said it was "*exceedingly good,*" or "*very* beneficial."

With the inanimate world—stars, moon, sun, ocean, and land, God stated His opinion: It is good. With animate life—animals and humanity—He gave a blessing. The purpose of the blessing was that this animate life would multiply and fill the earth. The blessing for humanity revolved around ruling the world well.

> God blessed them and said to them, "Be fruitful and multiply, and fill the earth, and subdue it, and rule over the fish of the sea and over the birds of the air, and over all living things that move on the earth" (Genesis 1:28).

---

* The Bible translations used throughout the book are my own. They are true to the original Greek and Hebrew texts of the Bible. My desire is to give a rich and expanded but accurate translation of what God has to say through His Word.

God's purpose, as stated earlier in verse 26, was that the earth should be governed; the blessing in verse 28 said that His divine desire and all-powerful providence would be unleashed to bring these good things to their designed purpose—and with the fulfillment of that purpose would come joy!

The purpose of God's blessing on Adam and Eve was to propel all of those good things in the direction of the couple's joy and dignity. Creation was like a big, wonderful box of toy blocks and Tinkertoys. God's blessing would arrange them in such a way that His children would thoroughly enjoy the gifts.

The Person of the Trinity who is given all ultimate credit for the beneficial creation with the blessing residing on it is the Son.

> In the beginning was the Word, and the Word was personally present with the God [the Father], and Divine the Word was continually. This One was in the beginning with God. Everything through Him came to be, and apart from Him not one thing came to be which became (John 1:1-3).

God the Son is the creator of all the benefits of life, and it was His blessing that rested upon all animate life. God is infinitely good; He is incapable of creating that which is not good; and His intention is that life should be benefited and fulfill its purposes. He who died for us is also the One who provided all good things.

This means that when it comes to temptation, compulsion, and addiction, it is a question of *management* and not nullification. The ever present question that a person who is struggling with temptation, compulsion, and addiction should have is, "How can I use what I'm experiencing in a healthy and good way?" (We would have to "uncreate" the world and dismantle ourselves so as to avoid temptation. That probably won't happen.)

Doris is a university student and a sex addict.* She despises what she has become; she despises who she is; she despises her existence.

---

* As is the case with a number of people whose stories are given in this book, Doris's actual name and circumstances have been changed to protect her privacy.

She despises the young men she gets involved with. She is also a Christian who is desperately ashamed of who she is—and oddly, yet not unusually, she despises sex itself.

She prays a lot. She wants her desires to be taken away. God won't do that. She does not want to be sexual; she deeply despises her body. God won't take away her sexuality. After all, He pronounced her body good. God won't destroy her, nor will He nullify her appetites. What He will do is attempt to introduce her to the proper management of her soul so she can enjoy what He has pronounced good and what He has blessed.

Doris cannot imagine—absolutely cannot imagine—a life where she is not replaying video clips in her imagination of illicit sex, a life where she can positively manage her sexuality and simply turn her mind away from impure or wrong thoughts. And that sense of despondency is precisely the problem. She feels so much a failure that escape seems impossible. Therefore, she is thinking about suicide to end her struggle. She wants to nullify and destroy the good things God has given her. We will see what happened to Doris later in this book, but in a word, nullification or death is not what God wants for us—but life and the management of what He has placed within us.

Creation as Christmas

Most addicts do not view the world and their bodies as a good place to inhabit. That is because of the deep pain involved with compulsion and addiction. What is common with addicts is not uncommon in the church.

All of life is a good gift. Yet in the church in the past and the church today, pressure exists to always reject reality, with its emotions and appetites, as a good gift of God. Sometimes the mind-set of the addict and the mind-set of the church are disturbingly similar.

If you observe certain churches, they function like they exist in an asexual world where only the really evil people have appetites.

They seem uncomfortable with appetites and appear to indulge in self-rejection. (Sometimes it almost seems that the only people who talk about food problems and sexuality are the sitcoms and magazines like *Hustler* and *Playboy*.)

Nervousness about human appetites is not new to the church. A blatant rejection of the body and the material world has happened in the past. During the third century, a religious leader named Mani had a powerfully negative influence on the church. Mani taught a form of *dualism*—that matter was evil, created by a lesser god, and that just spirit was good. Therefore, it did not matter what was done to the body because it was not important. Oddly, this led in two very opposite directions. Some then felt the body should be despised and roughly treated so it would not do anything wrong. Others felt that it did not matter what the body did, so sexual sin and indulgence was permitted. What both approaches had in common was a less than positive view of the human body and what was within.

Christianity, however, views creation as a divine Christmas morning. Let's merge Christmas morning with the creation story in our imaginations.

In our creation/Christmas story, God the Son—with great joy, explosive laughter, and a contagious smile—comes to the door of humanity at the time of creation. In a booming voice He shouts, "Let me in! It's your Christmas. Mine will come later! I have great gifts for you." We, humanity, come to the door and let Him in with great anticipation. Have you been around people who have a contagious laugh? God has one. The divine Son is laughing with anticipation at sharing His gifts with us. In this scene, we actually find ourselves giggling. (Kids giggle, you know.)

A great sack is over His mighty shoulders. Stooping down next to the tree (which He gives a thoughtful glance), He opens the sack. Immediately, out fly nightingales and sparrows. "That's just the beginning," He says. He brings out the gifts. A host of them involve food and recreation. Another gift is wine, to lighten the heart. Then, He sweeps His hand over us and grants the gift of relationships. Another sweep of the hand…and with a great laugh, He says, "I have given you the gift of sexuality. Have pleasure between yourselves. Enjoy the undercurrent of attraction and of life."

Then, a thoughtful expression comes across His face. His eyes look deeply into ours, and sympathetically He says, "I have a mystery gift for you—the gift of pain. It is a great and mysterious benefit. In time I will teach you its meaning and its use."

Lifting His arms over us with great dignity, He declares, "I empower all of these gifts to work for your benefit. The impulses of all reality will conspire for your blessing."

Then He laughs again and says, "Have fun."

THE GIFT OF PAIN

In the original creation story, in the Garden, our ancient parents enjoyed the gifts and got to know the Giver. Even though they were created as adults, they still had to figure out how they worked. Imagine that Adam was walking along and he stubbed his toe. The first human "ouch" echoed through the earth. Fascinated, Eve turned to him and asked what had happened. "The oddest thing," he said. "This sensation shot from my foot right into me and I instantly pulled my foot back." Then he said, "Well, I won't do that again. In fact, I will call that the 'I-won't-do-that-again' sensation."

Eve, who was very bright, took her toe and pushed it against the same rock Adam had stubbed his toe against. "What a neat invention. That feeling warns me when I press my toe against the rock, and it gave you the uncomfortable sensation so you wouldn't do the same thing again. That is clever."

Adam, who was also very bright, said, "Eve, I felt something like this…but different…before God fashioned you. When God asked me if I wanted any of those animals as helpers, a feeling came over me that I found uncomfortable. God told me it was loneliness. Loneliness felt a little like stubbing my toe, except it was deeper, longer, and more unsettling. When I woke up and saw you, loneliness went away and I felt wonderful."

Eve smiled affectionately. They both marveled at this thing called *pain.* They thought it was wonderfully clever. Pain reminded Adam to look for Eve. Pain kept Adam from stubbing his toe. Pain warned him when more pain might be coming. "What an amazing gift," they said.

Before the Fall, pain was a sensation; after the Fall, it was a catastrophe.

Our lives today are so often filled with struggle and inner chaos that we forget the original intent of the many gifts that are ours, especially the gift of pain. Adam and Eve said of pain, "What a neat invention." We say, "What a catastrophe!"

However, pain is what tells us we need to eat. Without that sense of pain with its discomfort, we would starve to death. Pain tells us that we are alone. As it weighs upon us, hopefully we will respond to its nudge or outright shove so as to seek the company of another. Without the pain of longing and desire, this world would never be populated, and the human race would cease to exist. Every desire has discomfort with it, and every painful physical sensation carries with it a powerful warning. That warning tells us that we must do something positive and wise to deal with the discomfort. But pain can be misused.

Misused Pain

When it comes to addiction and compulsion, pain is the critical puzzle piece. A pastor friend of mine, Mick Andrews, wisely said, "Addiction is the legacy of unaddressed pain."* His observation from working in the recovery ministry of his church was this: What was ultimately being mismanaged was pain. Pain was intended to

---

* Mick is the executive pastor at Sunrise Community Church in Sacramento, California.

wake us to the needs and threats of life, but addiction mismanages it. The equation of addiction is—

$$PAIN + PLEASURE = ADDICTION$$

God's intention was that pain should be a blunt but well-intentioned guide through life, much like a grumpy uncle who likes us but straightforwardly tells us when we are making a mistake or taking a misstep. Instead of listening to the grumpy uncle, though, we too often bury him under sugar and muffle his voice with pleasure.

Different Ways of Dealing with Pain

Alexander and Halaway did research on the use of heroin. In their article on their findings, "Opiate Addiction: The Case for an Adaptive Orientation," they noted an odd reality. Two people could be injecting or snorting heroin for six months, and then both would try to stop. One could, and one could not. They saw this over and over again. The time periods were sometimes different, but the results were the same. One was trapped, and one escaped. What was the difference?

They observed that the group that escaped had positive ways of dealing with emotional, relational, and physical pain. Coping mechanisms were present in their lives. Often when they were in pain, they would go to relatives and friends and work through the pain. Those who could not drop the heroin did not have alternative coping mechanisms, so they drowned the pain with a narcotic and experienced some pleasure. The deadly combination seemed to be as we noted above: *Pain plus pleasure leads to addiction.*

A lot of research has been done with high-school students to discover the difference between the students who are drug-resistant and those who are not. Common factors show up over and over again. Students who feel loved and good about themselves can stop smoking marijuana with what appears to be ease. Students who do not feel good about themselves or whose parents are going through a divorce or whose home otherwise has stress and strife cannot easily drop smoking marijuana. Over and over again the management of pain seems critical to the process.

In the introduction we mentioned the "no-bullets-flying therapy." Take away the stress and tension, and there was no need for the addiction. Take away the Vietcong threat, and the soldiers' hearts were free to be happy.

When we look at our culture today, we may easily conclude that many do not have an alternative means of dealing with pain. Alcohol addiction is up 50 percent in one generation—7 percent of the adult population, or 10 million people, are now problem drinkers. The practical ramification of that is, another four people are directly affected by each problem drinker. That means 40 million more lives are affected. The spillover is also that one-third of arrests are to be blamed on problem drinking. One half of highway fatalities are blamed on excessive drinking.

Marilyn and her husband would end each evening by drinking several cocktails. It tasted good and relaxed both of them. This was part of the fabric of their marriage. Then they became Christians. As they grew in their knowledge of the Bible and their participation in the life of the church, the evening habit continued. In some ways it was a point of pride that they were not legalistic. They had freedom in Christ to down some cocktails.

One Bible study organization Marilyn joined wanted to promote her to leadership. To her surprise, one of the rules was that leaders could not drink alcohol. She thought that was a bit much. However, she prayed about it and decided she would comply. As she started to stop her evening drinks, she immediately noticed something. The problems of the day did not drift away in the haze. The tension with relatives, the problems at work, and other stuff hovered like vultures. She was surprised at how handy the alcohol had been at keeping those vultures at a distance.

As she plugged away at keeping the rule of no alcohol, she was forced to pray more about the challenges, especially so she could sleep. She also chose to address the problems that nagged at her in the evenings. To her joy she found that prayer took away the tension and still left her with objectivity; the alcohol did not do that. She also found the courage through faith and prayer to address her daytime world. She no longer had the "mute button" of drinking. Now healthy pain and emotional discomfort could do their good work—the good work of telling her that something needed to be addressed in her life and relationships.

With the continual misuse of alcohol and food comes a whole host of adult health problems. The great majority of health costs are directly related to conditions that could be prevented. Diabetes, ischemic heart disease, stroke, cancer, suicide, broken bones, chronic bronchitis and emphysema, sexually transmitted diseases, and hepatitis are just some of the preventable conditions that flow out of succumbing to temptation, compulsion, and addiction. Addictive behaviors are a tragedy, but a preventable one.

What an addicted person does is like eating chocolate with their left hand to kill pain while scalding their right hand on the stove. As a solution to the scalding, it does not quite work.

The Pain of Unnatural Emotions

Pain was meant to be a good gift—warning us of threats, prompting us to seek food, relationships, and benefit, and reminding us not to repeat our mistakes. But when we succumb to temptation, compulsion, and addiction, a whole new host of pains is brought into our lives. Unnatural feelings we were never intended to experience come our way. Those truly unnatural emotions are *shame, guilt,* and *worthlessness.*

Many therapists and pastors who work with the addicted believe that *shame* is the ocean addicted people swim in. No one takes pride in having the predominate reality of their lives be sex, food, gambling, work, or something else. No one who is addicted wants to be viewed like Gollum in The Lord of the Rings, the creature who spent his existence pursuing a ring that would give him power.

As he fondled the ring or even thought of it, he would repeat over and over, "My precious, my precious." It is embarrassing to have the central experience of life be the next sexual encounter or the next meal. Surely we are more than that. But for the addict, with regard to themselves, they are not more than that. With that knowledge, shame envelops the soul.

Guilt also comes, for with the slavery of addiction has to come betrayal of others. The heroin addict may steal from parents, spouse, or friends. The sex addict may have no interest in others as persons, and implicit in immoral sexual encounters is always a betrayal of one's spouse. The workaholic sooner or later will realize that the God-intended life of relationships has passed by and family and friends have been betrayed by neglect in the process.

Worthlessness is the third unnatural emotion. On the home page of a Web site dedicated to Ana—the practice of anorexia—this statement was found: "If you feel you are the most worthless person in the world, come in—because within, you will find those who feel the same." Worthlessness is the feeling that I am not valued by others or myself. When, for instance, a woman finds that all the excitement she has in life is to go shopping, a feeling of personal meaninglessness sets in. "Is this all I am? Is this all I can do with my life? Are clerks in stores my only friends?"

If all of this seems strange to you, just imagine the most embarrassing moment in your life, the most shameful moment, and multiply that by a billion. That is where the addict dwells.

God did not intend for us to have those emotions, and he certainly did not intend that they should be the constant companions of many. Yet shame, guilt, and worthlessness make the problem of temptation and compulsion worse.

Several years ago I was giving a seminar at a church in the Bay Area of California on the core values of Christianity. The seminar was called "Setting the Heart Free" and it taught those core values from the book of Romans in the Bible. A couple was attending who never introduced themselves. They just sat and listened as I explained that God did not want us to live in shame, and one of the reasons Jesus died in our behalf is to take away from us any need to live life in shame. Instead we can confidently come to God the Father for help. The couple listened, the seminar ended, and I went on my way.

A year later that same couple came up with smiles on their faces to me when I was visiting the same church. They told me a striking story. The woman was a stewardess who went all over the world, and her husband stayed home with his own job. As she went away she would find herself involved with various men and become intimate with them. As she was away, her husband would engage in cross-dressing. He would dress as a woman and go out.

She would return to him and confess her wrongdoing, and after she was done, he would confess his own. He would say, "If you want me to leave, I will." She would say the same thing to him. Both of them were completely trapped. As they were telling me this, however, one of them broke into laughter and said, "We were so busy telling each other that we would leave, we never had time to leave." I thought their laughter did not match the seriousness of what they were describing, until the thought struck me that this was the laughter of the rescued and of the redeemed.

> The shame, the pain of it . . . was keeping them from the one true source of help, God. Take the pain away, and the addiction loses its strength.

They went on to say that at the previous year's seminar they had heard that Jesus Christ was not ashamed of them—not ashamed of calling them His brother and sister. In fact, His death on the cross was the basis for giving themselves radical permission to take what they were doing to God the Father and share it with Him so that they could find help in their time of need. As they began to do that, they found help. Their shame and guilt started to dissipate, and with that they found the courage to deal with their sins and their relationships. To their immense surprise, as the pain of shame went down so did the cruel control of the addictive behaviors in their lives.

What was a marvel to them was that the very shame their practices caused was the pain they were trying to bury and forget under the pleasures they sought. It was also the shame, the pain of it, that was keeping them from the one true source of help, God. Take the pain away, and the addiction loses its strength.

Beyond Anesthesia

There are many sources of pain in this life—some comes from relationships, some of it is physical, some comes from the trio of guilt, shame, and worthlessness. Wherever it comes from, the tragic mistake is to take a good gift of God and misuse it to bury pain and find some pleasure.

Using those gifts correctly, however, not only undercuts addiction but also unleashes the heart to truly enjoy the God-provided pleasures of life without shame and regret. All of us realize that life has its fill of good things. What we do not seem to realize is that when we truly enjoy ourselves, the heavens are happy. The Creator of all pleasures wants His pleasures to be delighted in. The inventor of pain wants pain to have its beneficial work.

What would life be like if we used the good things of life in a good way? The first thing we would experience is a depth of relationships that might have eluded us or escaped us. Temptation, compulsion, and addiction are the nonrelational way to experience the chemical treats that come with relationships. Certainly chemical benefits come from healthy relationships, but that is the minor pleasure—the great pleasure is the enjoyment of a particular person and special relationships.

Ultimately alcoholics and pornography addicts burn the bridges to relationships, but when the good things of life are not used as a substitute for relationships, the good people of life appear. Marriages become what God intended, a reflection of the Trinitarian God and the relationships among the three Persons of the Trinity.

Another crucial relationship is also discovered when the good things of life are not mismanaged. We are actually introduced to ourselves. Compulsive and addicted people find themselves to be bad company. Often they just notice their weaknesses, and they despise the person they have become. But as the fog of temptation, compulsion, and addiction is melted away by the sunshine of health, we can see ourselves clearly. We know our weaknesses well, but now we can discover our strengths and discover the person others and God love. I have often said that the gospel is God's means of introducing us to ourselves. For that introduction to take place, we need to deal with pain and not be captured by some misused pleasure.

When pain is managed and pleasures are controlled, then we will cease being afraid of what is inside of us. Talk to a woman who has tried dozens of diets and ask her how she feels about what is inside of her—the appetites, the will, the emotions, and the mind. She will say she is afraid of what is there. It is not her ally or friend. Instead what is inside is an uncontrollable nuisance. Lower the pain level and let her learn to truly manage her inner life (something we introduce in the coming chapters), and her fear will turn to respect. She will agree with King David when he wrote, "We are awesomely and miraculously made!" (Psalm 139:14).

When the good things of life are managed, we will learn to be cautious about temptation, compulsion, and addiction. We will respect them and know how to avoid them. We will notice the pain that empowers temptation, and then we will deal with the painful mood or situation quickly so our appetites do not carry us away. For instance, we will notice that when we are tired, we start "grazing" from the refrigerator.

When the good things of life are managed, then pain can do its good work. Pain will tell us when we are lonely so we will seek friends. Pain will tell us when we are ashamed or guilty so we will seek God.

Pain will become the gruff but good-hearted uncle God intended it to be. We have other "aunts and uncles," like pleasure, food, and sex, who are made for a party and stick to us like the best of friends. God does not begrudge us our pleasurable friends—indeed, His Son created them. He merely wants them tamed and beneficial.

⟿

Genesis 1 says that everything is good or beneficial, and that all of life is meant to be driven by the blessed purposes of God. In temptation, compulsion, and addiction, the good is bent away from its blessed purpose for something evil. However—and this is incredibly important—if we manage temptation, compulsion, and addiction correctly, all of life can become a treasure house of delight.

And as we use the gift of pain correctly, we keep ourselves from "doing the math":

PAIN + PLEASURE = ADDICTION

Of course, the equation also tells us we should lower the pain level in our lives. But it does not tell us *how.* There are additional realities we need to learn about. In this chapter we talked about how to view the pain within ourselves. In the next chapter we will see what is the primary truth we need to understand about God as we struggle with temptation, compulsion, and addiction. That truth will lighten our burdens and set our heart free.

TWO

Intervention à la the Apostle Paul

Pain is critical in the temptation, compulsion, and addiction cycle. Lower the pain and addiction's power loses its grasp. That is a critical and important insight. But there is a problem. Saying it does not make it so!

From toothaches to death, pain comes uninvited in many ways to many lives. We could tell a man to stop drinking himself to oblivion whose wife just died, but that would be like asking a rhino to do calculus. Or asking a person with a toothache to lower the pain will be difficult if that person does not go to a dentist. So it is true that lowering the pain is a critical principle, but it should not be reduced to a simplistic principle. Other realities are involved. Those realities come with the nature of compulsion and addiction.

Preoccupation with Desires

As a person succumbs to drinking or pornography or binging on food, they are giving into an impulse and a desire. That in itself is not a big deal. One impulse surrendered to does not an addict make. But as the mind begins to rely on the alcohol or the sexuality or the food to feel better and to have some pleasure, more and more of the mind becomes preoccupied with desires. Finally and eventually significant damage enters the life. Within this pattern are predictable emotions. Guilt, worthlessness, and shame take up residence. Powerful negative emotions sweep through the life. And the worst thing of all is the unnoticed loneliness. These accompanying emotions make lowering the pain more and more difficult.

Anorexia illustrates what we are talking about. Anorexia is a growing problem among young women and teenagers. The young woman may be simply starving herself, but telling her to stop most often does not work. But there is an addictive power to the problem. The emotions are very negative and powerful. A quote from a pro-Ana (Pro Anorexia) Web site will illustrate this:

> If you are half as **emotionally scarred** as I am, if you look in the mirror and truly **loathe** what you see, if your relationship with food and your body are already beyond "normal" parameters no matter what you weigh, then come inside. If you're already too far into this to quit, come in and have a look around.*

The emotionally poisoned were invited into the site for further damage. If the poison level is high enough, join, is the invitation. Inside the Web site the "Ana Creed" is written:

> I believe in Control, the only force mighty enough to bring order into the chaos that is my world. I believe that I am the most **vile, worthless,** and **useless** person ever to have existed on this planet.*

Real People Complicate Addiction

The tragedy is that the person who wrote about anorexia is not exaggerating; that level of pain is present. Part of the pain is again also loneliness. Shame drives a person into loneliness. Also loneliness is necessary to heighten any addictive experience. People and relationships have a way of cluttering up any addictive experience!

The reality of loneliness shows up always. A *New York Times*

---

* As found in the *New York Times Magazine*, 9/8/2002, p. 22.

reporter was talking to one of the young women involved with the Web site and she said, "What I'd like people to understand is that it is very difficult for people who have an eating disorder to go for help…I can't go to a doctor or a friend and ask for help. I can't tell anyone."*

Loneliness is painful. Under the best of circumstances, it is crippling. With temptation, compulsion, and addiction, it is always present. For by its very nature when a person is tempted, they have turned inward to an appetite to find relief and pleasure. Turning away from relationships, turning to one's own insides is what temptation ultimately is. It is not that an appetite is evil; it is just a poor substitute for a person.

Roberta loves her romance novels. She trades them with other women at work. She finds her mind is captured by reading them. If one of the handsome, charming young men described in those books actually showed up on her doorstep and invited her for a date, she would be frightened. That is actually what handsome charming men do to her: they make her nervous. So having a choice between a flesh and blood man at the door and her novel, the novel will win. Why? Because the man at the door has opinions, breathes, and has preferences. The tragic result for Roberta is that she is left lonely with an enflamed imagination.

Steve frequently visits pornographic sites. If one of those women pictured on those sites showed up at his door, he would be stunned. If she said, "I'll date you but I want you to be sympathetic and friendly and I want you to take my personality and mind seriously," Steve would decline the invitation, close the door, and go back to the computer. Real people complicate temptation.

As people head in the direction of temptation, compulsion, and addiction, they leave relationships behind. They do that unconsciously but with purpose. Also as the addiction hits, people start abandoning the addict. Who wants to live with an alcoholic? Who wants to lose money to 900 numbers or deal with the health issues of addiction? Very few. As shame increases, loneliness increases, and

* New York Times Magazine, 9/8/2002, p. 66.

the need for pleasure increases. Both the plunge into aloneness, and the refusal of friends and loved ones to stay around create a ruthless cycle.

But it must not be forgotten, addictions are just the normal struggles of the spiritual life; they are nothing particularly special. Our American culture is cowed by addictions, but they are a phenomenon as old as humanity. When Christianity had its start close to two thousand years ago, addictions had different names but the dynamics were all the same. Alcoholism and sex addiction were as common then as they are now. Early Christianity looked such things in the face, and smiled with confidence.

Truth That Rescues People

So now we come to the next strategic step: a critical truth needs to be grabbed by the person who is on the conveyer belt of addiction. No matter how quickly the conveyer is moving, nor what contorted position the person finds himself on that belt, a vitally important truth has to be grasped no matter how jarring and fast moving the conveyor belt is.

John was living on the streets, caught up in heroin addiction and male prostitution. He went through a sex-change operation and lost his family, job, and friends. He heard the truth we are talking about, and it changed everything. The truth in its simplicity shocked him, and its force pushed him into a new life. Hardly anyone reading this book will ever be in the quagmire that John found himself. But the truth we are talking about pulled him out. If it can pull John out, it can pull anyone out. Let's see what it is.

The truth we need to know is in the New Testament of the Bible in 1 Corinthians 6. It is a remarkable passage because Paul the apostle approached addiction in a way that is as modern as tomorrow.

Corinth was a city of temptation, compulsion, and addiction. Corinth in Greece was a major port city of the Mediterranean world. People from all over the ancient world lived in and went through the city. It was known as a rich town with very loose morals. In fact, the Greeks took the name Corinth and turned it into a verb, Corinthianize, meaning to live a sexually immoral and debauched or loose life.

Paul the apostle, a proclaimer of the new religion Christianity, set up churches within the city. As soon as he did, he ran into the problems of the culture: moral collapse, deep animosities within the community, and unbridled sexuality. This was the reign of paganism, and paganism of the worse sort. Being a Greco-Roman city, the populace worshipped many gods. One of those gods—or more precisely, a goddess—was Diana. An aspect of her worship was sacred prostitution. A male could go to the temple and hire a prostitute, and the sex and the fee was considered worship. In our secular society sexual immorality is viewed as a choice. In this ancient culture, it was viewed as a religious obligation.

In the early evening as the men were going home from wherever they worked in the city, the sacred prostitutes of Diana would fan out and offer themselves to the passing men. We might complain about the invasion of the Internet into our homes, but this was far more intrusive. Such practices were considered a normal and accepted part of life. Morality was a mess!

When he received a letter from the church he established, Paul was gone from the city. The letter described the growing morally chaotic condition of the church, and they asked for his help. His response was the letter we know as 1 Corinthians. The church asked about the Christians who were still involved with this sacred prostitution, who were getting drunk, who were thieves, who had other moral problems. They asked: How should they view them and what should they do to help themselves?

Stage One: Condemnation

To answer that Paul wrote 1 Corinthians 6. The beginning issue in the chapter was that several in the church had taken their legal squabbles to the pagan law courts. Paul found that abhorrent because the individual believers with the help of the church community should be able to sort squabbles out. He then accused them of missing the reality that spiritual truth changes lives! He reminded them that heaven was in the business of changing lives.

> Do you not know that the unrighteous will not inherit the kingdom of God? Stop allowing yourselves to be deceived; neither fornicators, nor idolaters, nor adulterers, nor homosexual prostitutes, nor homosexuals, nor thieves, nor the greedy, nor drunkards, nor revilers, nor swindlers, shall inherit the kingdom of God (1 Corinthians 6:9-10).

The kingdom of God is the future inheritance of believers. In that kingdom there will be no sin. Their lives will be so incredibly transformed that no variety of evil will be present in God's kingdom. The sordid status quo is not acceptable in heaven. Since that is our future, our present should be conforming to that hope.

As soon as these words from Paul were read in the Corinthian church meeting, I am sure a level of discomfort went through the room. The person who was secretly involved in an affair became guilty and nervous; the greedy felt dismay; the drunk became nervous; those who had done wrong felt wrong. Paul listed the more flagrant sexual sins but then he went on to include those of a more pedestrian or common variety: such as greed and sarcasm (the reviler). In one way or another, everyone in the room who was clear minded and listening probably felt some discomfort. The natural response through the congregation would be to feel shame and guilt.

Paul by his list implicitly rebuked those who were taking each other to a pagan court. Right before those verses about the kingdom of God, he concluded his address on the issue of going to court by saying, "On the contrary, you yourselves wrong and defraud, and that your brethren!" (1 Corinthians 6:8). So we know that Paul was condemning the parties going to pagan courts to find restitution, but he was also pointing out what else was unacceptable.

Nearly everything he mentioned is on the temptation, compulsion, addiction continuum: fornicators, adulterers, homosexual prostitutes, and homosexuals are involved in being tempted, compulsive, and addicted. All end in sexual addiction. Drunkards obviously represent alcoholic addiction. Thieves and swindlers represent an arousal type of addiction; they seek excitement and are hooked on it. It is risk- taking at its most extreme. Revilers are the aptly called rageaholics; they approach relationships with a chip on their shoulder. All of these categories are present in today's congregations as well as in the ancient world.

Stage Two: Confusion

As he described who will not be in the kingdom of God, probably the listening congregation shuddered with discomfort. Those who were especially prone to an honest conscience must have had some sense of guilt. As they were considering their failure and guilt, Paul added to the stress by saying something that on the face of it would appear confusing. He wrote,

> And these some of you were, but in contrast you were washed, but you were set apart or sanctified, but you were justified in the authority of the Lord Jesus Christ, and in the Spirit of our God (1 Corinthians 6:11).

"We don't feel particularly washed or sanctified," would be the hidden admission bolting through their hearts. "How could we be sanctified?" those who were struggling with alcoholism asked in their hearts but not out loud. Out loud would have been embarrassing. Those who were visiting the prostitutes thought, "No possible way were we washed clean! We're enslaved!"

From the greedy to the drunken, a wave of confusion washed through the listening congregation as Paul's letter was read. Paul had achieved his goal. On the one hand, he wanted it to be crystal clear that God wanted no part of a sinful lifestyle. On the other hand, he wanted to shock the congregation so that they would take a fresh look at what their salvation meant. His goal was to create short-term confusion so they would be led to ask, how can a person who has such moral failings be washed, sanctified, and justified?

As I go from Bible conference to Bible conference, either in the United States or outside of it, I meet Christian after Christian who is very aware of their sin or wrongdoing, but who is inevitably much less aware of what Christ, the Holy Spirit, and God the Father has done on their behalf. The condition of the Corinthian church has been replicated ten thousand times over in the lives of our contemporaries. Christians today are superbly aware of what they do wrong, and grossly unaware of what God the Father has done for them.

Joe was a Christian who struggled with alcoholism. I taught a seminar in his church on what he had in Christ, and I also taught the principles that were such a powerful force in delivering believers from addiction. As he applied the truth and it changed his life, his motto almost became, "Why hasn't anyone told me this before?" He had been suffering the same sort of confusion that the Corinthian church went through.

Stage Three: Deliverance

After getting the attention of the congregation, Paul went on to tell them how to deal with the problems of temptation, compulsion, and addiction. As we enter that section, we need to slow down and think about how Paul wrote his letters. Often those letters were what is called "dense writing." Dense writing is when every word is significant, and what is written needs to be read several times over.

In the early church, the epistles or the letters from the apostles were read out loud over and over again. In the ancient world the sending and receiving of letters was a huge deal. Often when a family would receive a letter, they would invite in their relatives and friends and read the letter over and over again. The writer of the letter would "pack" in as much as possible in the letter and the recipients would "unpack" as much as possible out of the letter. That is precisely what Paul and the Corinthian church did.

The contents of chapter 6 have to be looked at carefully and slowly especially since it has such abrupt transitions. Paul transitioned to the topic of temptation, compulsion, and addiction quite quickly. After describing how the Corinthian believers were washed, sanctified, and justified, he wrote,

> All things are permissible, but not all things are profitable. Everything is permissible for me, but I will not be taken under the authority of anything (1 Corinthians 6:12).

This turn may seem abrupt to the reader or listener, but the new topic was completely aligned to what he had just written. In verse 12 he told his listeners that all things were permissible but not all things were profitable. And in the next verse, he told them what he referred to.

God Is in Favor of Our Bodies

Paul's topic was food and sexuality and their relationship to the body. Food was for the belly and the belly was for food. But such things will not be forever, because God will nullify the need for such in His future. Also the body was for the Lord and not for sexual immorality.

What Paul shared was a profound Christian truth that all the appetites have their source in God. The appetites may be deeply misused in this world, but the creator of the appetites is the Son of God Himself. That being the case the use of the appetites was encouraged. But they should be used profitably, and they should not be allowed to become enslaving. Appetites were morally neutral as gifts of God: It is what we do with them that matters. Nevertheless, one has to be careful, so Paul declared that he would not allow himself to be placed under the authority of his appetites.

Then, he went on to describe that God was the ally of the body and was for it. As practical proof of that Paul offered the truth of the resurrection. God has such an interest in our bodies that He will raise them from the dead. So at the beginning of the section, Paul wanted his listeners to be sure that God had nothing against human appetites and He was all for the human body.

When it comes to compulsion and addiction, these truths are vitally important. We have seen with those struggling with anorexia that body hatred and despondency over the appetites exist. When a person who is struggling with temptation and addiction fails time after time, inevitably an intense dislike for the body erupts. Paul did not want the Corinthians to fall into that trap. Instead he wanted them to view their appetites as God's manageable gifts.

He raised the issue of the proper management of the body at the beginning of the section so that the Corinthians would feel that the problem was not obliterating the body but the management of the appetites of the body. After developing that thought, he went on to say *how* the Corinthians with all their problems were washed, sanctified, and justified.

Our Connection with Christ Is Here to Stay

Paul asked them if they knew that their bodies were the members of Christ. He did not ask them selectively. He did not say, "Don't those who are doing everything right know that their bodily members are the members of Christ?" Nor did he say, "Don't the alcoholics know that their bodies are the members of Christ?" Nor did he ask, "Do not the greedy know that their bodies are the members of Christ?" He asked all of his listeners right across the board (those who were visiting prostitutes and those who were not), were they not aware of that truth?

Since their bodily members were the members of Christ, Paul then asked the question: Should the members of Christ be used in an illicit relationship with a prostitute? Naturally the answer was, absolutely not! Yet at the same time, Paul was answering the confusion and the questions that his previous comments raised. The question that was raised was, how could those who are involved in various forms of immorality be washed, sanctified, and justified?

Paul's first answer was that the Christian involved in immorality did not lose his identity in Christ. Therefore, the reality of what God has done in Christ did not disappear in the face of sin. Justification has given the Christian the righteousness of God in Him (2 Corinthians 5:21) and sanctification has permanently set apart the Christian to God. Boldly Paul made the Christian's union with the prostitute a union with Christ also. That truth, in a most concrete way, said that the profound differences that Christianity has brought into the life were there to stay.

> Most Christians feel that if they perform—live righteously—then God will bless them. It is "barter-system Christianity." But what Paul is saying here is profoundly different.

As we go further into the passage something needs to be pointed out that is uniquely powerful. As Paul developed the subject, he first pointed out the privilege that grace has given the believer, and then he presented a standard for the Christian to meet. In the first part of 6:15, he wrote,

> Don't you know that the members of your body, are the members of Christ?

Then, he asked the question that presented the moral standard:

> Therefore, then, shall I take the members of Christ, and make them the members of a prostitute? May it never be!

Paul affirmed the privileges of the Christian before he underscored the moral expectations that a Christian should meet. This is quite contrary to how many Christians think and instinctively live. My observation is that most Christians feel that if they perform— live righteously—then God will bless them. It is "barter-system Christianity." But what Paul was saying here is profoundly different. He wanted the Corinthian Christians to have a sense of how richly they have been blessed. He wanted them to start with the blessing of God and not with the expectations of God. With Paul the path to God's blessing is not through being moral, but instead it is through discovering what blessings God the Father has provided in Christ. The morality comes as a result of accepting the blessing of God.

Connection at the Deepest Level

However, Paul was not ignorant of the reality that though the union with Christ existed there were other unions in this world. He went on to say that the one joining himself to a prostitute became one body with her, a real union existed. With that he used the reality of the marriage bond from Genesis where Adam and Eve became one flesh. They became closer than any other human relatives.

But again in the face of that, he pointed out another reality that already existed:

The one joining himself to the Lord is one spirit (2 Corinthians 6:17).

This is very similar to Paul's statement that we are one body with the Lord. Now he made the statement that we are one spirit with the Spirit. That of course again was a recognition that God has already provided for the Christian. The Christian did not have to gain the spiritual benefits through a moral life or after ethical performance.

Also another implication existed. Whenever I teach these verses to a group, I always ask, "This is not a trick question, but what is closer to God—flesh or spirit?" The group looks around suspiciously wondering to each other what the trick is, and then I repeat the question, "What is closer to God—flesh or spirit?" Finally, one brave soul will say, "Spirit." The person is of course correct. Even though there is a union with the flesh of the prostitute, nevertheless, a deeper union existed and that is with God's Spirit.

So what we see so far is that the Christian who may be having moral difficulties has not lost his union with Christ, nor his union with the Spirit. This union with the Spirit has to go deeper than any union with the flesh. Below temptation and failure, a deeper level exists within a person. That awareness of a deeper reality is often a source of pain to the person caught up in addiction because it speaks of a different and better reality. But that deeper level also means that we are more than our appetites.

Our Bodies Are God's Love-Gift to Us

After pointing out the greater and deeper union that a believer has, Paul went on to give moral encouragement. He told the Corinthian Christians to flee sexual immorality. Notice again the imperative for the moral life flows from what a Christian has already, and not what a Christian could obtain through moral endeavor.

Then Paul made this most interesting comment on the human body:

> Every sin which a person might do is outside of the body, but the sexually immoral person is continually sinning against his own body (1 Corinthians 6:18).

The body that is misused in compulsion and addiction, the body which is enslaved to appetite and moods, the body which is weakened by mismanaged sexuality, work, and stress has its rights. It can be sinned against. If it can be sinned against, then it must have inherent worth and value. Paul has already told us that God was for the body; that God's love for the body extended beyond the grave because the body will be raised in the resurrection. This body also was joined to Christ. Surely we have a spiritual union with God but also a physical union exists between Christ and our bodies.

The body was important to God because it is the physical representation of who He is. But the body is also important because it belongs to us and God loves us. As persons we were made to be physical representations of the divine. That representation will go on into eternity itself: We will always have a body.

This emphasis on the significance of the body is in great contrast with addiction. The body in addiction is a nuisance: it is a repository of weakness and pain. For many who are caught up in addiction the only way out is to kill the body by suicide. In Christianity the body is a great gift, and a place where our union with God is played out. The body was intended to be a source of great wonder and awe. David, the Old Testament psalmist, wrote,

> I will give thanks to You, for I am awesomely and miraculously made; wonderfully miraculous are Your works, and my soul knows it very well (Psalm 139:14).

This psalm was given over to describe God's creative work in weaving the body in the womb, and to describe the majesty of a person's creation. The body was meant to be a miracle and a source of great delight to those who inhabit it. Therefore, the body does have its rights.

Jane knew that life nor God ever intended that she would be living for her prescription pills and her next drink. Deep within she felt the frustration that came from knowing that life should be more than just depression and various means to melt away pain. Even though she knew that something deeper existed for her, she did not know how or what would break her out of the cycle of defeat. That is why this chapter in 1 Corinthians is so important because it contains what Jane needs to know and everyone needs to know.

PAUL'S GREAT ADDICTION-BREAKING TRUTH

At this point in the letter, Paul gave the great truth that should never be forgotten no matter where a person is on the temptation, compulsion, and addiction continuum. He has been talking about the significance of the human body, and now he shared the crowning truth:

> Don't all of you know that your body is the inner sanctuary of the Holy Spirit which is in you all, which you have from God (the Father) and all of you are not your own (1 Corinthians 6:19).

No matter where a Christian is in sin and addiction, he or she cannot be closer to God than they are right now. That is the liberating truth! Now let's examine further how Paul actually said that in his letter.

Notice first that he was addressing everyone in the church. In our modern English Bibles, it is sometimes difficult to notice when the writer is addressing the individual or the whole group. In Greek he was clearly addressing the entire congregation, and that is why I use "all of you" in my translation.

Our Bodies Are the Holy Spirit's Living Room

What is it, then, that all of them share in common? Each of their bodies was an inner sanctuary of the Holy Spirit. The word inner sanctuary did not refer to the entirety of the temple, but it referred to the particular spot where God dwelt in the Holy of Holies. The ancient Temple of God in Israel was a complex of several parts: first there were courts for the women and men, and finally an inner court for the priests. In the furthest reaches of the priestly court was the Holy of Holies where God dwelt, the inner sanctuary.

Once a year for about a half an hour the high priest or leading priest went into that inner sanctuary to meet with God and deal with the sins and uncleanness of the people of Israel. An incredible privilege was given to the high priest. He among all the people could be in the direct presence of God; he represented the people to God.

But here is a fundamental reality, Paul did not say the Corinthian Christians were high priests or even priests. He said that the believers were the inner sanctuary itself. What are the differences? The high priest entered the presence of God once a year but the inner sanctuary was always in the presence of God. The inner sanctuary could not be closer to God than it already was.

The priest could only go in and out; he could not stay. No chairs or benches were anywhere in the temple. Always the priests left. The high priest had to be extra careful that he was ceremonially clean. If not, he could be harshly judged by God with death. The inner sanctuary, however, was always in the presence of God. It was always being graced by the presence of God. That was what the Corinthians were.

We have to slow down and really digest this truth. It's incredibly important. Nowhere in the Old Testament were a people told that they were the Holy of Holies. Rites and practices, barriers and walls kept the people from the immediate presence of God. The most privileged man in the Old Testament was the high priest: His privilege lasted 25 minutes a year!

Today it would be similar to someone saying, "I am so close to God that I'm always on his lap." What it said to the Corinthians was: "You are always in the presence of God. You cannot get closer to God than you are right now. You cannot leave the presence of God."

An inner sanctuary by definition was where God dwelt. This was also a very strong statement of the deity of the Holy Spirit. The third member of the Trinity was in every Corinthian believer. God the Father sent Him to be with them. The authority of heaven has approved His presence!

Paul Turns the Tables on Addiction

For the Corinthians everything now was turned around. Paul started off by telling them that no sexually immoral person, drunkard, greedy, or impure person will have a place in God's kingdom. And he said that the Corinthians used to be that, but now they were washed, sanctified or set apart, and justified. In his explanation of that Paul told some compelling truths:

1. *You do not lose your body.* It will be raised in the resurrection.

2. *You do not lose your identity.* Even joined to a prostitute, the Christian's bodily members are the members of Christ.

3. *You do not lose your connection.* We are one spirit/Spirit with God.

But the greatest reality of all is that we do not lose the presence of God: We are the inner sanctuary of God. The great truth is that a Christian cannot get closer to God than he or she is right now.

For many Christians in compulsion and addiction that is absolutely counterintuitive. They feel worthless, ashamed, guilty. To them God feels like He is beyond the highest heaven. With that sense of God's withdrawal is the accompanying hopelessness and helplessness. Such emotions, Paul was telling the Corinthian Christians, were an illusion. They cannot be closer to God than they were right then!

What goes on with the typical Christian when sin and addiction comes? The typical believer is like a person who is walking toward a wall. As he walks, God the Father is walking with him with His arm around the Christian's shoulder. The Christian comes to a wall and pushes his face right up against the wall. As he stands there he starts moaning, "God has deserted me because of my sin. Nowhere is He to be found! I have sinned. I am guilty, worthless, and a bum. I am not worthy of the High and Holy One who inhabits eternity."

All the time the Christian is doing this, God's hand is tapping him on the shoulder and saying softly, "I can't leave you or forsake you. You are the inner sanctuary." The Christian mutters as he pushes his face more and more into the wall (while God is tapping his shoulder), "Quit bothering me! Don't you see that God has deserted me because I am a guilty, worthless sinner."

Then he hears a majestic, powerful voice say, "Wherever you are I am there. Before you have arrived at your most humiliating moment, there I am waiting for you. You cannot abandon me nor can I abandon you."

The most important message that a Christian can hear as he or she is being tempted, or in compulsion or in addiction is God is there with you in the Person of the Holy Spirit.

Good Riddance to Hopelessness

It is in these last few verses that Paul made the clearest statement on the reality that makes all the difference. A Christian is never abandoned by God no matter where they are in this life; nor is anyone without hope in this debasing and lonely process. Hopelessness is part of the emotions that accompany addiction, and if God does not desert the addict, then hope has no reason to leave.

It is not sin nor shame that defines the reality of God's presence. The defining reality is that the believer is washed, sanctified, and justified. Jeff was snorting cocaine and feeling miserable. Alienated from his family, he was in a motel room alone. Needing more and more cocaine, he also drank and overate. A Niagara Falls of anesthetic was being poured into his heart, and it was never enough. Thrashing around on the bed, he noticed the Gideon Bible. As he thumbed through the first few pages, he found a section titled "God's Comfort." Having been raised in church, he knew how the chapters and verses worked. He found Hebrews 13:5-6. (Here I give my translation, not the King James):

> Without the love of money let your manner of life be, being content with what you presently have. For He Himself has said, "I will absolutely never leave you, and absolutely I will never abandon you." So that with continual confidence we can be saying, "The Lord is my great helper. I shall not fear what a man shall do to me."

Jeff had heard those verses before but they came with a divine power. He felt the presence of God in the motel room while the white powder was on his upper lip. Jeff thought that if this is truly the powerful sense of God's presence that he has, then he can deal with this or any challenge. Before it had never occurred to him that God could be present in the mess that his life had become. It had never occurred to Jeff that God the Father actually wanted him to be real and not religious. But here was God's promise and here was God's presence.

With God's presence an actual enthusiasm came into his life to make it different. Years would go by before I met Jeff in the seminary where I taught. Those were years where the struggles were very real and failures happened. But the sense of God's involvement and care sustained him through the process of changing his life.

The God of Our Worst Moments

In one sense God is a "tasteless friend." Seemingly He is endlessly tolerant about those who come to Him for help and endlessly patient in waiting for those others to recognize the need of His help. But He has a solid foundation to do just that. His Son died for each person so as to deal with the issue of wrongdoing; the Spirit of God washed every one who has come to Christ; God the Father has set apart for Himself all who trusted His Son as children under His constant care, and finally each and every child of God has been justified with God's righteousness which means they are infinitely accepted and never rejected.

What Paul was doing all through 1 Corinthians 6 was to address those with addictive problems and tell them that they did not need to get more of God but instead they had to use what they have already been given from God. The human heart seems to assume that we first need to do the heavy lifting, and then God will get around to doing His part.

After telling them the privilege that they have, he made the application that they no longer belong to themselves (6:19). This was made even more explicit as he wrote,

> For you have been bought with a precious price, indeed then immediately begin to glorify God in your body (verse 20).

Since all of those realities were so, Paul commanded the Corinthian Christians to grab hold of the truth that has been told them and as a result, present a positive picture of who God was by their lives. But they were commanded to act because of what God the Father has done for them through Christ. At their worst moment, God gave a Son for them. They were worth a Son to God as is.

They did not have to morally clean up, and religiously perform to have had Christ die for them. Without asking their permission, He died for them:

> God recommends His own delighted passion [*agape* love] for us in that while we were continually sinners Christ died for us (Romans 5:8).

God's goal is to meet us where we really are and then as He delivers us to take us where He and we would like to be. Notice the list of truths Paul shared:

1. *We do not lose our future.* Our bodies will be resurrected.

2. *We do not lose our identity in Christ.* Even in fornication or sexual immorality our identity is secure.

3. *We do not lose our connection.* We have been joined to the Spirit of God.

4. *We do not lose our closeness.* We cannot be closer to God than we are right now because we are the inner sanctuary of God.

5. *We do not lose our value.* We are worth a Son to God.

That is the message that those in addiction need to hear: God never abandons His own. Wherever we are in failure, He is there to help.

The "recovery movement" is the term used for those who work with people struggling with addictions and compulsions. Within that movement the leaders are always encouraging the people who are struggling to start their recovery immediately and do their recovery "one day at a time." The addict has to give himself or herself radical permission to start immediately and dramatically. They have to be desperate enough to take the plunge.

The message the recovery movement is giving is: act today, start today, change today. The interesting thing is that any addict or compulsive person or tempted person has *to act like* God is immediately at hand in order to get help. What Paul did was to give radical permission and express reasons why to do so. God does not abandon His own: He is always there for them.

The Non-Abandoning God

In some ways this is a hard truth for people in our culture to accept. Abandonment and betrayal is as common as people. So the truth of a non-abandoning God seems completely counterintuitive. When Paul started into his subject with naming the people's failures and also the impossibility of such sin being in God's kingdom, they did not expect him to lead them into such assuring truth. Everyone who has experienced abandonment and abandoned others who disappointed them would not have expected such faithfulness to the morally failing.

Yet such faithfulness is the essence of Christianity. The Son came to save the sinner, so the sinner's job description was simple, be a wretched sinner. When a person trusts in Christ, he or she is given the righteousness of God in Him. Righteousness is the essence of the relationship abiding in the Trinity. The Trinity infinitely accepts one another and never rejects one another. That is what God's righteousness creates for us: we are infinitely accepted and we will never be rejected.

How this works out practically for the struggling person is that God's Person and help is available wherever they are and whenever they need it.

For the individual who has no religious preferences but has a spiritual interest, this same message from 1 Corinthians 6 applies. All of God's loyal affections described in the chapter are available to that individual. All that has to be done is to ask God for help while accepting what Jesus Christ has already done for us. He died for all of our wrongdoing without asking our permission. He took away any reason we might have for staying away from getting to know God the Father.

THREE

The Cycle of Addiction

When it comes to defeating addiction, we have examined two critical realities. First, unaddressed pain is a crucial element in pushing people into the slavery of addiction. And second, wherever a person is in their descent into the slavery of addiction, God is radically available to help. This help does not have to be earned or deserved. It just has to be asked for. Since addiction is also a series of interconnected challenges, this help as it comes will have to address more than just pain. Understanding and dealing with the central role of pain is critical but pain begins an entire addictive process that needs to be taken apart a piece at a time.

Now we are going to place pain in the larger context of what is called the addictive cycle. This is very important because mismanaged sexuality and food addictions develop within a process. Understanding this process and coming to terms with it spiritually will open a person's life to a vitally healthy spirituality. The following diagram will play a key role in what we discuss in this chapter and later on.

PAIN (NEGATIVE MOODS)

▼

DISASSOCIATION

▼

FANTASY WORLD

▼

INITIAL ACT

▼

ACTING OUT

What Happens on the Outside

On the outside, in the external world, the process appears straightforward. It starts out with a very normal habit of life such as eating or sexuality: harmless enough appetites. But as time passes for some the habit begins to pattern the rest of the person's life. For example, the appetite for food begins to go beyond the normal limits and now menus are being written throughout the workday. All of us who do some cooking need to create a menu or two but it is a completely different story when thinking about menus and eating consumes the workday.

In the evening a woman may begin to binge eat, and then to keep her weight down, she uses laxatives to purge herself. This becomes an increasing pattern. The normal habit of eating is now taking on a life of its own. Her appetite is managing her and she is not managing it. People have noticed at work that she seems to have a greater interest than most in what she eats, and also her thinking and conversation seem preoccupied with it. From the outside the person appears to becoming compulsive. Her thinking and conversation revolve more and more around food.

As the habit patterns the life more and more, and the thinking becomes more and more compulsive, noticeable damage begins to invade the life. Social relationships are being ignored. The woman is going more into isolation to binge and purge. She talks less to her friends. This is where addiction sets in. The patterns and the compulsion become addictive when damage enters the life and the person cannot step back. They *accept* the social and physical damage. That is addiction.

> The patterns and the compulsion become addictive when damage enters the life and the person cannot step back. They *accept* the social and physical damage. That is addiction.

Joe, a young college student, goes out with women and enjoys their company. But this very normal aspect of sexuality has begun to change. He fantasizes more and more about his women friends. At the same time he is viewing pornography on the Internet. As time passes his fantasies take more and more time during the day and the Internet takes more and more time at night. The young women notice that Joe is starting to make some crude sexual comments. Even though at the college the women are used to blatant sexuality something is different about this. They can't put their finger on it, but it makes them uneasy.

Joe's grades are being affected. Everything in his imagination invariably goes in the direction of the endless sexual videos being played inside of his brain. Sexuality has patterned his life. Using other language, eroticism has set in: Sexuality has invaded areas of life where it simply does not belong.

What is going on within him is compulsive, and what other people are noticing is the overflow of his inner life. But the damage is the addictive part of the problem. His mind has become just a video player for the X-rated; his study time is sharply reduced; his sleep is affected; his grades are lowered; his relationships are subtly affected. Addiction is the damage that compulsion causes. Joe is now addicted because he cannot pull himself back from the personal damage in his life.

Step #1: Pain

Much can be said about how lives are affected by addiction, but the real area of struggle is in the inside. It is the internal addictive cycle that has to be understood. With that understanding a person struggling with temptation will know where to devote the energy and efforts. And if the efforts are directed in a wise way the end result will be a huge leap and improvement in the person's spiritual life. This knowledge is hugely important. Not just important for a struggler with addiction but for every person who wants to live life to its full, and enjoy all the good gifts that God has provided.

The first step in the addictive cycle is having unaddressed pain in the life. We have mentioned pain previously but now we need to place pain in a full context both as it relates to a person's inner life, and as it relates to the Bible. Both psychology and the Bible have a lot to say about unaddressed pain in the life.

When Pain Is Not Dealt With

The pain can either be emotional, or physical. But what is important is that the person does not try to solve the emotional problems through relationships or the physical pain through a physician. Instead an appetite is tapped to drown the pain and give pleasure. The first reality in the addictive cycle is pain.

Now when we see the word pain, we need to broaden what we are looking at to include those things that would normally not occur to us at first. If we asked Joe, what is the pain that led him to indulge in enslaving pornography, he would have to think a long time. Then, maybe even after a day or two, it may dawn on him that all the discomfort that he was experiencing was simply boredom. Boredom! That does not seem enough to alter a life and cause an internal implosion. But it did. Normally when a dike collapses, it starts with a very small leak and expands over time until whole sections of the dike collapse and disaster happens.

Judy had been a closet alcoholic for years. She was 42 and a professional graphic artist. If you asked her what was the unaddressed pain in her life, she also would have to spend a day or two thinking. She would also have to visit a therapist. After a lot of thought her answer would be simple bitterness. She was unhappily married and her anger at her husband had become low-grade bitterness. She hardly ever noticed that it was there. But she had been drowning that bitterness for years. The alcoholism had been going on so long she initially had no idea what the initial pain was.

With George it was more straightforward. It was the bullets in Vietnam. He knew the cause for his heroin addiction. When he was shipped home, he actually found it easy to drop the heroin. He was as surprised as anyone else. "Everything I knew told me," he said, "that I was in trouble." Instead, to his relief, the desire for the drug dwindled over a few short months.

Whether the unaddressed pain is obvious, as with George, or hard to pinpoint, as with the others, that is where the addictive cycle begins. Like the pilot light in a gas oven, unaddressed pain is always there ready to ignite.

Pain and Negative Moods

The issue of unaddressed pain is also often unaddressed in evangelical Christianity and the other churches. But such is a critical category within the Bible, and especially in the New Testament. Paul taught the flesh had two weapons, and what he had to say needs to be thought about carefully.

> They who are owned by Christ have crucified the flesh-system with its painful moods and appetites (Galatians 5:24).

Notice in my translation, I have taken the word that is often translated as "passion" from the Greek that Paul originally wrote in, and translated it as "painful moods." Often a problem in translation occurs because a given English word like "passion" does not quite fit the Greek word. That's the case here. Please bear with me as I develop the meaning of this word. It is greatly important not only because it is so overlooked but because it opens a whole new world of spiritual understanding and growth.

The Greek word is pronounced *pathema*. If we take apart the word, we'll notice *path* within the word. *Path* is found in some very familiar modern words. Pathos comes from *path*. Pathos is an overwhelmingly sad emotion engulfing the person. Pathetic comes from *path*. Pathetic means to be so emotionally overwhelmed by the problems of life that one is crushed and defenseless. *Pathema* is given this meaning by a lexicon (a foreign language dictionary): "(1) as what happens to a person and must be endured *suffering, misfortune* (HE 2.9); usually plural *sufferings* (HE 10.32); (2) as strong inward emotions, only plural *passions, impulses*." Obviously what we have in Galatians 5:24 is "strong inward emotions." These are emotions that envelop the person.

We have a great example of the meaning of this word from a document that was written at the time of Jesus and Paul. It was Fourth Maccabees, a work in Greek probably written by a rabbi. The purpose of the book was to show how knowing the law kept a person from being controlled by *pathema,* or strong powerful inward emotions. What is helpful about this book is that it underscored how important it was in the ancient world to deal with "passion," or as we are going to call them, "painful moods." In his first chapter, the rabbi gave a definition.

> Many are the things which belong to moods *[pathema],* such as pleasure and pain. For before pleasure there is appetite and after pleasure joy.
> And before pain is fear and after pain sorrow. And rage is a common mood with pleasure and pain.

The rabbi defined the word positively and negatively. In the first part of the definition he gave what he thought were the elements of the process of "negative moods." They started with appetite, and then the appetites went after satisfaction. The other part of the definition was entirely negative: The "negative mood" is pain, fear, and sorrow or depression. At the best it is a sense of lack and need, and at worse it is painful depression. I have decided to wrap all of this in the phrase "negative moods." The mood could be the sense of deprivation expressed in longing or it could be straightforward emotional pain.

How Negative Moods and Appetites Interact

So let us return now to what Paul the apostle said. He stated that the flesh or flesh-system had two weapons that it used. One we are very familiar with if we attend church and that would be "appetites" or desires and lusts. One cannot help get the impression, at least in church, that at any moment appetites are ready to ambush and carry off the Christian into unbridled licentiousness. But the flesh has another weapon, negative moods, painful states of deprivation or discomfort. Paul assumed that appetites and negative moods working together were the great challenge the Christian faced.

Let's take two other examples from what Paul wrote of how these terms were joined together. In this way we will see that we must not only consider what is going on in our appetites but also in our emotions:

> Do not live your life in the painful moods of appetite, even as the gentiles do who do not know God! (1 Thessalonians 4:5).

Notice that the two terms are intimately related. Paul said that the Thessalonians should avoid building their lives around the painful moods that belong to appetites. In one sense, he was saying that one was encapsulated in the other. When an appetite of the flesh captures someone, within the heart of that appetite was a sense of pain or deprivation or both.

Linda has been sleeping around. She seems to get quickly involved with guys sexually and then just as quickly she leaves them behind. If we could go behind the mismanaged sexuality and see what was at the heart of these short sexual liaisons, we would find a sense of worthlessness (a profound pain) and loneliness. The sexual relationships were involved with so quickly Linda hardly had time to notice the pain, but pain was there.

Peter had grown up in an abusive home. The dad was an angry alcoholic and the mom was fixated on watching "soaps" all day. Peter was 19 and he just assumed that his background was normal. He also assumed that the low-grade depression he lived in was normal too. He had never known anything else. The thought would never occur to him that the endless hours he spent on the Internet had anything to do with the pain that he was carrying. Yet at the heart of the addictive preoccupation with the Internet was depression.

Linda and Peter illustrated Paul's point. Negative moods, a sense of deprivation and emotional pain, were at the heart of their struggles, and at the heart of the mismanaged appetites of the flesh were painful deprivations. In both Galatians 5:24 and 1 Thessalonians 4:5, Paul linked negative moods and appetites.

Let's take just one more example, and this will be from another of Paul's writings, Romans. In the first chapter of Romans, Paul described how God has turned humanity over to its own insides. Previously, as Paul described it, humanity had rejected a personal relationship and knowledge of God in earth's ancient history. As a response, since humanity wanted no part of God, God turned them over to what was driving them, their own insides:

- "God handed them over to their appetites" (Romans 1:24).
- "God handed them over to dishonorable moods" (verse 26).

What was significant about these two verses is that there were two major areas of difficulty with humanity. One, the obvious one, was appetites. The other word was the one that is becoming more familiar to us, moods. These are the twin challenges from the flesh, that independent power of selfishness within, the twin challenges of mismanaged appetite and painful or negative moods. For Paul seemingly the kernel or the heart within mismanaged appetite was the negative mood. The negative mood could have two aspects to it:

painful deprivation or painful emotion. Either way the individual was left with either low level discomfort or screaming pain.

This perfectly matches up with the addictive cycle. In the addictive cycle before the seduction of mismanaged appetite comes unaddressed inner pain or deprivation. Talk to those who are involved in sexual or food addiction and they will freely admit that they exist in plenty of pain, but they may not be able to explain that the heart of mismanaged appetite is the preceding state of pain. Ordinarily they do not notice pain because they leap quickly into the quest for relief. Pain often is omnipresent in addiction, but the order and primacy of that pain may be overlooked.

Living in a Culture of Pain

What makes the pain of the individuals we have introduced even worse is that they also live within a culture of pain. On the college campus one can see this readily. In the general culture, people often are moving too quickly to notice. This culture of pain produces deep discomfort within millions, and then it seeps over to enflame the addictive cycle. This culture of pain particularly is entwined with sexuality and food.

The title of this book is *Sex, Food, and God*. It is particularly interested in looking at how the struggles with sexuality and food relate to God. Those two become great challenges because of unaddressed pain in the life. Many individuals are of course in plenty of pain, but we also live in a culture that delivers pain by the boatload. As we try to come to terms with mismanaged sexuality and food, the issue of unaddressed pain is crucial to understand and address.

Part of that unaddressed pain comes out of the culture itself. To deal with that pain, we must understand what the world is doing to us. When we look at what the culture tells women and men, the answer is not much of anything positive. But what little it says is devastating, and produces monstrous pain.

Our non-profit teaching organization works frequently with college and university students. With the students we have found significant levels of pain driving much of the addictive behaviors that we have seen. Much of this pain comes from what the culture is throwing at these students. The messages are brutal.

Our culture's message to men. Men are being told today that all they are is their sex drive. The message hits them everywhere they turn. The Internet, TV, radio, everpresent advertisements, simply say over and over again, "All you are is your sex drive." I won't bother to prove that this statement is true. Just go out and line up 20 young men and ask them, What is the one consistent message that this culture repeats over and over again? As they work through the possibilities, it will always end up at the same place, sex.

Those who watch Howard Stern on TV or listen to him on radio may ask, "What is so bad about that?" An *awful* lot. Almost any young man has dreams and expectations. Almost any young man wants to be respected. Look at the army recruiting advertisements directed at young men. They do not say, "Come and be your sex drive." Instead they say, "Come and become a man you can respect, come and achieve, come and become greater than yourself."

But that is not what the general culture says. The message "All you are is your sex drive" gets connected to the male gender. The young person or the older male begins to define himself that way instinctively. That begins to produce a pain that is the universal negative mood in addiction, shame. No one would want to be defined as merely a drive, but that is what the world does to so many.

Then something worse happens. Every time the young man may have a romantic impulse or sexual interest, shame sets in. So then the pain of shame is present. If this does not seem realistic to you or you are a woman, let's see what the culture does to women and compare it to the message the men are getting.

Our culture's message to women. Women hear something different. Our culture says to them, all you are is how you look. You are just your appearance. Personal worth and everything that goes with it is connected to how pretty the woman is. Since very few women actually feel good about how they look, their appearance becomes a matter of shame. The same difficult emotion of shame that the men are feeling is now the emotion the women are feeling. Their identity is connected to their appearance, and then in one more step it is connected to what they eat. Because the cultural message is that how you appear is dependent on how you eat. As a result, the appetite for food becomes a source of shame and discomfort.

A president of a sorority at a university in the state of Washington told me a story about young women and food. She said that she has seen a scene repeated over and over. At the sorority three or four women would sit down for a meal together. As they ate, the women would watch the prettiest woman at the table and carefully watch how much she ate. None of them would eat more than the prettiest. They would be too embarrassed to eat more than the prettiest did, she said.

Shame for many women gets connected to their appearance and further gets connected to food. So when they look at food, they look at it differently than men. When certain women feel a desire for food, they instantly feel shame over their appearance and feel nervous about the food. When certain men feel sexual desire, they feel ashamed over the desire and embarrassment about who they are. Both genders are placed in pain, and then that sets them both up for the addictive cycle.

The utter irony is that the women may deal with the pain of shame over food by eating more. The men may deal with the pain of shame by becoming involved with more and more mismanaged sexuality.

Pain is what starts the addictive cycle. The connection to pain is something the Bible recognized, and Paul the apostle particularly pointed that out. In our modern culture sadly pain and shame has been directly related to the two major appetites that people experience. The culture says that men are just their sex drive and women are just their appearance. Not only does that set up the genders for the addictive cycle, but it also sets them up for strained relations.

How can young women and men comfortably relate when they are carrying such discomfort? They cannot.

We shall see in later chapters that God does not reduce anyone to the drives within. In fact, the Son came to rescue us from that insanity. We shall see that God the Father has an absolutely different perspective on who we are. The genders are defined differently by God, and this difference can turn almost anyone's life into poetry. We shall see what that ennobling vision is in later chapters.

So the addictive cycle starts with pain. The pain may be subtle such as shame, loneliness, or boredom. Or it may be brutal such as high anxiety and bitterness. But regardless what the pain is, over time the person becomes habituated to start the addictive cycle when pain appears.

Step #2: Disassociation

What researchers have found is that the first response to the appearance of pain or discomfort is to step out of relationships—or as they call it technically, *disassociation.** That is the second step of the addictive cycle. The individual may be in the midst of a crowd but withdrawal takes place. The focus of the heart leaves the people around it and concentrates on the desires and thoughts and imaginings within.

The important reality behind disassociation is that it will heighten the experience of pleasure. People and relationships have a way of distracting. So to heighten the pleasure others have to be excluded. This transition can take place in a second.

Unfortunately again, what is going on in the culture reinforces the rush into isolation of the addictive cycle. Many in our culture have found relational isolation a way of life.

In healthy homes when a child would experience pain, the young child would go to the parents and be comforted. Over the years the young child will experience comfort thousands of times. So when

---

* *Disassociation* is not to be confused with *dissociation*. The former emphasizes stepping out of relationships. The other emphasizes stepping out of consciousness of self.

the child becomes an adult, he or she will instinctively go looking for someone to talk to about the pain. The person from a healthy home will be more inclined to deal with emotional pain relationally.

The individual who has grown up in an unhealthy home or even an abusive home will have a different set of instincts. When the child in an unhealthy home was insulted by a brother or sister and would go to a parent, the parent would either ignore them or unfeelingly tell the child to toughen up. After thousands of experiences of being ignored or being lectured, the child is trained not to go looking for people to share his or her pain. When this child becomes an adult, they will already have all the training they need to go into disassociation. Since the person does not deal with the negative moods or pain through relationships, the pain then will not go away. So the next step is of course to use a mismanaged pleasure to drown the pain.

These types of family backgrounds create one of the great false-hoods of addiction that since the pain would not go away that means that it will stay forever. Since emotional pain normally is reduced and dissipated through relationships, the person who has not experienced dissipation will not expect relief. Such a belief will reinforce the drive into mismanaged pleasure.

At a Campus Crusade conference I was speaking at, a young man approached me who just short weeks before had left a cocaine habit and converted to Christianity. He was obviously frightened and anxious. He said that he had been clean just for some weeks, and he was expecting to fail and go back to a life of addiction. He was feeling tense, and he did not expect it to go away but it would just get worse and worse and finally the unending pain would force him back to drugs. He did not have to tell me how he was raised. Obviously he had been well trained never to expect that emotional pain would ever go away.

As I talked to him, I explained that there are hundreds of millions of people throughout this planet who, when they feel tense or are in emotional pain, honestly expect it will dissipate and go away as they relate to people. I talked to him for a long time. I emphasized that his fear of the pain not going away (so that he will be forced back into addiction) was largely life or family background training. And the life training did not match reality as it really works. I could tell that he was not at all convinced. So I made a point also of telling him that failure is not a big deal in Christianity. "When failure comes," I said, "get yourself back to God the Father and keep on heading for health. Christianity is designed for the failures, not for the healthy."

So two reasons exist for why people go into isolation: One reason is to heighten the experience of the addictive behavior, and the second reason, that is what some people have been trained to do.

Step #3: Entering a Fantasy World

The next step after pain and disassociation is to step into a supporting fantasy world. So the pattern that is developing is as follows:

NEGATIVE MOODS

▼

DISASSOCIATION

▼

FANTASY WORLD

What has been noticed by those who work extensively with the compulsive and addicted is that as people plunge into the world of mismanaged desires, they begin to buy into a completely false set of beliefs in order to sustain the flight from relationships and the world outside.

Joan has been going to her weight reduction group for five years. She has not lost an ounce. Dutifully every meeting she is weighed with her shoes off. She's never disheartened by the news that nothing has changed. Her sincere belief is that she's metabolically incapable of losing weight. Asked about walking a half hour a day, she states with conviction that exercise simply does not work for her. What she does not say is that part of her regimen is visiting her hidden snack drawer at work. (No one but the whole office knows about it.) Also right before bed she snacks, and she sincerely believes that evening snack will not affect her weight.

Joan also has just been told that she is on the verge of diabetic problems, and also she needs to be concerned about her heart. What she says to herself is, "I'm still young. Those problems happen later." Her age is 46.

Whatever avenue of inquiry we could pursue with Joan, she will have a response that she thoroughly believes. Asked why she continues with her weight reduction group, she will say with complete sincerity that is how you lose weight. All of those questions though just deal with the mechanics of weight reduction. More significant realities are going on.

Joan's parents were a cold lot. When she had a problem, they told her to solve it herself. Encouragement and compassion were not present. Her mom only had endless self-pity for herself. So when Joan had a problem, she did not go to anyone, but she quickly discovered that food made her feel better. After years Joan did not realize that now the slightest emotional disturbance would send her in the direction of food. She had learned the first two steps of the addictive cycle. She had unaddressed pain, and she would disassociate. Eating was her closest friend. But to stay grossly overweight, she needed more than that. She needed a set of false beliefs to sustain her practices. She had them.

The Fantasy World's Purpose and Effects

The further a person goes into addiction the more they will need a false world, a fantasy world, to sustain them. When divorces occur, and jobs are lost, those harsh blows of reality will need a parallel universe to keep the person from admitting the truth that their life is really out of control. Oftentimes the beliefs are completely absurd. But the fantasy world serves a purpose, it justifies the rush into appetite.

The fantasy world also affects how we view ourselves, the world, and God. Those realities will be affected since they impinge upon the rush into addiction. The belief about God for Joan, a very sincere Christian, was that weight had nothing to do with spirituality. Joan was partially right. Her weight would not increase or decrease God the Father's love for her. But what she chose not to believe or notice was that her unaddressed pains were spiritually significant, and the Bible taught very strongly that such pains should be taken to God. But in her mind, her God had no interest in such things. She also chose to believe in a world where calories did not count; diabetes would not overtake her, and medical problems affected everybody else but her.

Concerning herself, she sincerely believed that if she exercised calories would simply not be burned up. When it came to her weight, she believed in a "pre-scientific world." Deep, deep inside she also believed she had no willpower. Further, she also struggled with worthlessness. She believed the cultural messages that a female's worth is based upon her appearance. Did she have all these beliefs when she was much younger? No, but as time passed, she needed this fantasy world to keep herself enslaved to food.

Tom also had a fantasy world that he existed in. For Tom that world did not include God because he was a practical agnostic. Nevertheless, his world had a distinctly false picture of himself, and also a false picture of those who inhabited his world. Tom was addicted to sex. He honestly believed that it was normal to always be somewhat sexually aroused. In fact, he could not imagine existing without a compulsive preoccupation with sexuality. For him being human was having a continuous current of sexual videotapes flowing through his mind. If that would stop, he honestly felt he would cease to exist.

He worked at a Costco, and went to school. He did not notice that he had very little ambition, and whenever the thought struck him that he was taking forever to get through college, he would drown the discomfort under a flow of sexual images. Nor did he notice the pliable women in his fantasy world did not quite match the women he worked with and went to school with.

The dimensions of his world were pretty limited. He was casually dating Peggy. He liked her and he was sexually involved with her. Every once in a while he would have the disturbing thought that pornography was so much more interesting to him than Peggy. He could not explain why; it just seemed strange. His view of the world was such that women were confusing to him. Real ones did not match the fantasy world women.

The Inner World Becomes Self-Contained

The further a person goes into addiction, the more illusions the thinking has. Why should that be so? It is because the person's world is almost entirely self-contained. The most important thing in the internal world is the sensations of pleasure and expectation of pleasure that the person is experiencing. Nothing is closer to the person's heart than the feelings within. That atmosphere and those sensations carry their own sense of reality.

Connected to the sensation are pictures of anticipation. And in the anticipation the person is already feeling the consumption of the food or the sexual experience. Those sensations are the person's reality. Sustaining those sensations are the self-justifying perspective and the memories or pictures from the past that guarantee that these same sensations can be experienced certainly in the future. Because these false beliefs do sustain the intense internal experience, it seems perfectly sensible to keep on believing them.

The internal world of the person is a little bit difficult to grasp, but maybe this comparison will help. What if I tried to convince you that the world did not exist? I told you that the trees outside your window were not really there. I went on to tell you that the people who were talking to you were just holograms. You would question my sanity. In fact, you might start pounding on the table in the room we are standing in and say, "This table is here. This room is here! And this world is here."

The world of the addict is just as real as the external world that we were talking about, except the addict's world is much smaller. While pounding on the table to prove that the room exists may make a point, the addict has something far more validating than the table in the room. The addict has a continual flow of sensations that is closer to the heart than the room he or she is in, the air being breathed, or the fist against the table. The continual flow of sensations, the images connected to those feelings, and the anticipations being produced by memories of previous pleasures—those make up the addict's world.

> The continual flow of sensations, the images connected to those feelings, and the anticipations being produced by memories of previous pleasures—those make up the addict's world.

It is as real to the addict as the non-addict's experience of the external world. To keep these sensations flowing the addict needs to believe more and more fantasies. It is almost like the Mad Hatter said to Alice in *Alice in Wonderland,* we have to believe two impossible things before breakfast. That is what the addict has to do. When the obvious evidence is entering the life that the appetites are taking a greater and greater toll, the addict needs a belief system that justifies the trip on the tollroad.

Yet in some ways, it is easy to understand why these untruths are so easy to believe. They are continually supported by the sensations and emotions within the body. Therefore, when the addict actually begins to consider the damage and contemplates change, everything that they will need to believe and do will be utterly counterintuitive. Nothing within them will want to believe that a life without the addictive behavior is possible.

The Most Dangerous Element

In one sense, the fantasy world is the most dangerous and

powerful element in addiction. That is where the real struggle is at and where the empowerment for the appetites comes from. For example, a man from a healthy background intuitively understands that when he feels strong attraction for a woman he is working with, he can wait it out and it will pass. The intense attraction will pass. The person from an unhealthy background and who is entering addiction will have the opposite thought: This sensation will never pass. So instead of going passive as the first person did, the addictive person will feed the sensation until it is completed one way or another. That false belief sustains the addictive behavior.

It is also the fantasy world that will say that there is no help in sharing with another human being. "Communication solves nothing!" will be the belief. For the healthy person, the belief will be that communication can solve almost anything. So the addicted person will intuitively disassociate while the person from a healthy family background probably will not.

So the middle part of the process is the most strategic and the most dangerous.

PAIN (NEGATIVE MOODS)

▼

DISASSOCIATION

▼

FANTASY WORLD

▼

INITIAL ACT

▼

ACTING OUT

Five parts exist in the addictive cycle, but it is the step in the middle that is central to the whole process. Unfortunately the recovery movement often will strongly address the other four elements but leave the crucial center alone. It is the false world that gives permission for the pain to be unaddressed. It is the false world that encourages the person to go within himself or herself. The false world so enslaves the person that the next two steps of the addictive cycle are absolutely inevitable unless the ground opens up and swallows the person, or the woman has a heart attack, or the man has a pistol placed to his head. Hardly anything will stop the next two steps when the fantasy world has been entered.

Fourth and Fifth—The Initial Act and Acting Out

The whole addictive cycle is designed to not tax the heart's attention but instead to allow the mind to completely focus on the appetite and satisfy it. So as the man or woman initiates the activity the action has to be simple and straightforward. It has to be robotic.

Jane starts the process by going shopping for food. She is embarrassed by the binging and purging she does. So she actually goes to three different stores and gets a gallon of ice cream at each one. That is her initial action, and when she does it, it is completely robotic. That is important because as stated it does not interfere with the anticipated pleasure.

George's initial act is to simply turn on a computer. Everything else follows that. He then proceeds to pornographic Web sites. The whole process is mindless because the mind is utterly preoccupied with pleasure.

Both Jane and George then complete the acting out. This series of actions are repeated over and over again. Mindlessness is what is needed. The state of pleasure that they are seeking is actually pretty fragile. Both of them do not realize that they are severely restricting their lives and their world is becoming more and more narrow.

The fragility of what they are doing is shown by how easily the whole process can be interrupted. If a person walks in on George, he would immediately turn the computer off. Or if a friend walked up to Jane in the store and started talking, she would not pick up the ice cream as she would normally.

Now the recovery movement normally emphasizes the last two steps of the addictive cycle. That is the easiest part of the process to interfere with. Oftentimes the recovery movement will try and completely restructure the person's life. The line that is standard is, "Go to 30 meetings in 30 days." The reason for that is so the person will plunge into a complete change in life. Further, a sponsor is often provided to get the person through. That obviously again will help the individual restructure her life, and it will also address the issue of disassociation. A companion has been provided to relate to through the process.

The last two parts of the addictive cycle are significant, but they are not central. The fantasy world is the heart of the cycle. No visitor or rescheduling of a life will penetrate that. Only the person caught up in the compulsive chemical bath of desire is the one who can change what is being believed and perceived in those depths.

So let's summarize what we have examined. Temptation, compulsion, and addiction fall into a predictable pattern. Two dozen or so different habits can become addictions. This pattern is called the addictive cycle:

The Addictive Cycle

1. *Unaddressed pain in the life.* Negative moods or physical pain, unless they are addressed through relationships, and in the case of physical pain medically, can train a person to seek pleasure as a means of drowning the pain.

2. *Disassociation.* In order to heighten the pleasure experience, the person will step out of relationships, and focus on the anticipated pleasure.

3. *Fantasy world.* People will support this pattern by choosing to view themselves, God, and the world is such a way that participating in the cycle seems almost reasonable. This fantasy world will be a whole system of false beliefs that will be continually reinforced by the pleasure that the persons are expriencing. Such pleasure ultimately is their world.

4. *Initial act.* Whatever the habit is, it will begin with a robotic, mindless action that sets the person on the path of gratification or obtaining the pleasure that is so wanted. The goal of the initial act is to not interfere with, but instead to heighten the pleasure for the person.

5. *Acting out.* Then, the person completes whatever the action is that will guarantee the pleasure. It could be the use of heroin or sexual intercourse with a prostitute.

After the satiation of the sought-after experience, pain simply has to arise again to send the person down the path to the pleasure that will drown the negative moods or pain. Then, this pattern will be repeated over and over again thousands of times until the person either dies or finds something powerful enough to interfere.

We have stated that the fantasy world is what holds this whole process together. Feeling some painful emotions, stepping into loneliness, initiating a simple act, and then completing it are not realities that demand much of the mind or person, but what really does demand the mind's surrender is buying into the fantasy world of false beliefs. Those beliefs have incredible power.

In the next chapter we are going to examine some of those false beliefs and also some of the incorrect perspectives that Christians and non-Christians have about temptation, compulsion, and addiction. The chapter will be critically helpful because it will isolate some of the mental habits and perspectives that empower addiction.

FOUR

What You Don't Know... Can Enslave You

We have seen how central the fantasy world is to the addictive cycle. Experiencing pain, stepping into loneliness, a robotic initial act, and acting out are either things people experience or things people do. They involve experience and action and not necessarily perspective or thought. But it is the fantasy world that brings those elements together into a menacing combination called the addictive cycle. The fantasy world is how those trapped in addiction intuitively see themselves, the world, and God. Included in that are particular beliefs that buttress or support the false world that the person inhabits who is heading into addiction. Some of those beliefs come from our culture and some of those beliefs are within the Christian churches.

These incorrect beliefs have to be dismantled. What inevitably happens as an individual or a Christian works through the issues of addiction and compulsion is that they discover they have dangerous misunderstandings.

Misunderstanding #1: "It's Not That Big a Deal"

One of those dangerous misunderstandings is expressed in the sound of an easygoing voice that says lightheartedly, "Temptation, compulsion, and addiction are not a big deal." They do not view addiction as a sometimes deadly affliction.

A devil's alliance almost exists between those who are lighthearted about temptation and addiction and those who are uncomfortable with the recovery movement within the churches. In a mirror reflection of the lighthearted, the eyebrows of those who have not struggled with compulsion or addiction can be quickly raised by those who take such things as addiction and recovery seriously. The eyebrows are raised at conservative churches, synagogues, and mosques. In those institutions what you know and what you do is central, and the struggle with addiction is viewed as peripheral or almost unnecessary if a person knows and does the right "stuff." The non-addicted eyebrows can be raised by the recovery movement, and with a mocking voice the church person might say, "Hello, I am Joe, I'm a sex, food, fun addict."

It's Only Food

Also in the general culture, addiction may not be taken seriously, a dangerous misunderstanding. Let's take one specific illustration of not taking addictive behavior seriously, the overeating of food. Six years or so ago, I went with my daughter to a weight reduction program. She wanted to try it, but she did not want to go alone. Her friends turned her down so she asked me. I was delighted to go. Our daughter was just coming out of her teen years, so to be invited along anywhere was a high privilege for a parent. Most of the time I was the only male at the program. After we were weighed in to see how we were doing, we would have to listen to a lecture.

We attended for several months and my daughter did not lose any weight, but I lost nearly 25 pounds. I listened to woman after woman share how they were incapable of losing weight and the true success story was few and far between. At no time did any of the lecturers come out and say that some of the women might be addicted to food. Yet examples of addictive behavior abounded. For example, one young mom described how she threw a party for her young daughter. She had baked a cake, and the kids at the party only ate half of it. She then wrapped the half of cake in plastic wrap, and then put aluminum foil around that. She took the cake out to the trash and then threw dirty diapers over it. An hour later she went back to the garbage can, and dug out the cake, unwrapped it, and ate the whole thing. She told the story to illustrate how powerful the draw was to overeat, and how powerless she was against it. But the woman did not use the word "addiction" nor did the lecturers. At no time in the meetings did anyone talk about the addictive nature of overeating. Yet interestingly all the aspects of the addictive cycle were mentioned randomly. But the addictive cycle as such and the power of the fantasy world were never addressed directly.

I do not think this group was unusual. Weight was the problem to be solved, but the central issue of addiction, and the reality of the fantasy world, were never consistently or clearly addressed. To be fair they had a poster on the wall saying, "Issues in Weight Loss: identity." But that poster was never mentioned, and identity or the picture we have of ourselves was never addressed.

What was mentioned endlessly was counting calories. One of the more spectacular moments was when a lecturer spent half an hour going over low calorie desserts to the delight of the ladies. As she was going through the various recipes, I felt that the room was soon to erupt in dancing over what was shared. What should have been written over the front door is: "All who enter here must make calorie counting their life!"

This entire experience struck me as group meetings to put Band-Aids over deep, bleeding wounds. No one was mocking the idea of overeating as addiction, but by the very approach they were reducing addiction to a numbers game. Get your calories down and the weight will go. The heartbreaking reality is that overeating is a matter of identity, a fantasy world, compulsive sensations in the mind, and the challenge of changing an entire lifestyle.

Further, severe medical issues are involved including shortening one's life. Pursuing the person who is severely overweight is a variety of illnesses that may involve nearly every organ in the body. The heart especially is put at risk by such behavior.

The word addiction was never mentioned but also unmentioned, as one would expect with a completely secular organization, were the spiritual issues involved. Unaddressed pain in a person's life, disassociation, and a fantasy world or false identity are all spiritual issues. Further, the initial act and acting out are certainly moral issues and spiritual ones.

Some groups do approach overeating as an addictive behavior, but those groups are rare. Watch TV and check to see how many weight loss programs and special diets mention any addictive issues at all. By that very lack they are communicating a lighthearted approach to, for many, a life dominating and heartbreaking problem.

Harmless Recreation?

The culture also has a flippant approach to mismanaged sexuality. I was watching a situation comedy several days ago. It was genuinely funny. At one point the central couple walked in on the woman's niece making out with a young guy on a couch. The man was incensed, and a semi-humorous exchange took place and the young man left. Several minutes later he returned, knocked on the door, and when the door was opened, there he stood holding a condom. The laugh machine took over, and chuckles supposedly came from the audience. After the door scene, a harmless advertisement came on.

What would have been more appropriate would be an advertisement or two on genital herpes, and the drugs a person needs to take to deal with it. In those drug advertisements the talk is about embarrassment, some shame (not much), and the medical problem of STDs.

Kaiser Permanente, the nation's largest nonprofit medical provider, and the Centers for Disease Control, the most prestigious medical research organization in the United States, consider promiscuous sex as medically risky behavior. They consider someone who has 50-plus sexual partners as being medically at risk. That person does not necessarily have to have a sexually transmitted disease. It is the sheer numbers alone that create the problem.

For human beings there is no such thing as harmless sex. We are persons who bear within ourselves everything we have done in life and everything that was done to us. Our soul carries our life's history impressed deeply upon it. We are a composite of what we experience. Our inner life is wrapped around our experiences. To lower sex and food to meaninglessness is to reduce our relationships and our pain to meaninglessness.

Misunderstanding #2: "Addiction Just Happens"

Most people, including this one at one time, felt that compulsion or addiction just happens. No rhyme or reason exists for how it works. But in the previous chapter we have seen that the addictive cycle starts out with unaddressed pain, emotional or physical. We have largely focused on emotional pain because physical pain should properly be addressed by doctors.

But research, massive research, has shown that addiction has a certain *logic* to it, as enunciated in the addictive cycle—and certain *locations* for it to erupt. The locations are twofold: first adult situations that are stressful, and then stressed-out families. Addiction often shows up in adults who have been raised in certain types of families. These families are usually stressed or highly dysfunctional.

Stressed-Out Families

For years our educational nonprofit, Becoming What God Intended Ministries, has presented a community outreach called most recently, "Creating a Healthy Family" and before that "How to

Overcome a Dysfunctional Family Background." Much of what is in the lecture is based on my personal experience, and on hundreds if not thousands of conversations with people. One of the many conclusions that are presented in the lecture is that young people growing up in dysfunctional homes either drown their painful emotions by repressing them or drown them under addictive practices.

Of course that could be dismissed as just based on personal experience and anecdotal stories, not solid research. At the same time, as we presented the "Creating a Healthy Family Lecture" we were met with dismissive disagreement from some pastors and church members. They thought all we were saying was so much "psychobabble." They did not feel that understanding one's family background mattered.

A most graphic example of that kind of resistance occurred with a very large church in Arizona. The church leadership, particularly the senior pastor, did not want to use the title, "How to Overcome a Dysfunctional Family Background." He did not like the word dysfunctional. So we eventually agreed on the title, "Creating a Healthy Family." (I was not pleased at all. I jokingly said to our team, maybe we should call the outreach, "Sinned-Against Sinners, Come and Get Sanctified." That title would guarantee that no one would show up. In fact, I would not show up myself!)

So we went with the new title, and the megachurch put a mouse-like amount of energy into promoting the lecture. Afterward a member of the leadership team called to tell me not to feel bad about the poor effort by the church. She said that the pastor's lack of enthusiasm was the reason. She said ironically that the senior pastor had been raised in an alcoholic home and he did not permit anyone on the very large church staff to either discuss that or refer to it. His view was that no one really needed to understand one's family background but it was just the Bible that was needed. Naturally I agree that the Bible is desperately needed all the time.

I feel, however, that understanding one's family background is key for dealing with many of life's issues, and also key to understanding much of what the Bible has to say. But in the conservative evangelical churches that we largely dealt with, the response was mixed at best.

Coming Up with ACEs

In the last year, however, we have come across a medical study that has completely confirmed what our team has been saying for the last 15 years. Kaiser Permanente Hospitals and the Centers for Disease Control joined hands for a research project in San Diego, California. In the late '90s, they did the largest research project in the history of the world on how family background affects adult health.

Eighteen thousand people, all patients of Kaiser, were involved in this study. Again the largest group ever studied. The study was called the "Adverse Childhood Experiences" study, or the ACE Study. The average age of the population was 57. What the researchers did was ask the individuals to fill out a four page single-spaced questionnaire about how they were raised, and how was their health as adults. They particularly asked them about different adverse conditions growing up. The conditions are listed below with the percentages of people who, according to their responses, fit with each category.

Household Dysfunction	Prevalence (%)
Substance Abuse	27%
Parental Separation/Divorce	23%
Mental Illness	17%
Battered Mother	13%
Criminal Behavior	6%

Abuse	
Psychological	11%
Physical	28%
Sexual	21%

Neglect

Emotional. 15%

Physical. 10%

What is very important to bear in mind with this list is that the average age of those who filled out the form in the late '90s was 57. That means they grew up during the Eisenhower presidency, and they were born in the 1940s on the average. This explains why the divorce rate was 23 percent. During their growing-up years the divorce rate was half of what it is now. Also the sexual abuse rate for both genders averages out at 21 percent but in actual fact it was 24 percent for the women and 18 percent for the men.

In our nonprofit ministry we have thought that emotional neglect was a critical factor to consider in evaluating one's growing-up years. When Kaiser and the CDC did their research, they stopped in the middle of the project to reevaluate carefully what they were doing. At that point they added the category of neglect, both emotional and physical, to their study. They had concluded that those two also deeply influenced adult health.

They compared what they learned about the growing-up years, and examined what actually happened to the physical health of these adults. They have been able to generate an astonishing amount of data from this information, and many medical journal articles have come from it. They have come to some solid conclusions concerning family backgrounds and addiction. First, Adverse Childhood Experiences (ACEs) are common. Second, ACEs are very strong predictors of later health risks and diseases. Third, this combination of factors makes ACEs the "leading determinant of the health and social well-being of our nation."*

Climbing the ACE Staircase

With each of those ten factors, those doing the study would credit the participant with one ACE factor for each category that was indicated by the questionnaire the person filled out. Forty-

---

* V.J. Felitti, PowerPoint lecture.

eight percent did not have any ACE factors; 25 percent had one; 13 percent had two; 7 percent had four or more. More than half had at least one, and if one factor is present, there was an 84 percent likelihood of others being present.

Then, they took these ACE scores and compared them to the respondents' adult health, and they discovered this about addiction: "Addiction highly correlates with characteristics intrinsic to that individual's childhood experiences."* In other words, addiction does not happen randomly but it is directly related to stress in the home, or unaddressed pain in the home.

What they found is that as the ACE score went up the percentage of those suffering from various addictions went up. Let us look at some examples.

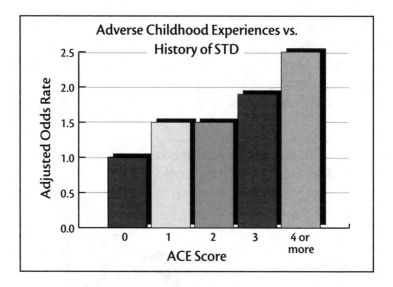

As the ACE score increases the incidence of sexually transmitted diseases goes up. The presence of STDs obviously would be an indicator of sexual addiction. Notice in the following chart the direct correlation between the ACE score and adult alcoholism.

---

* Felitti lecture.

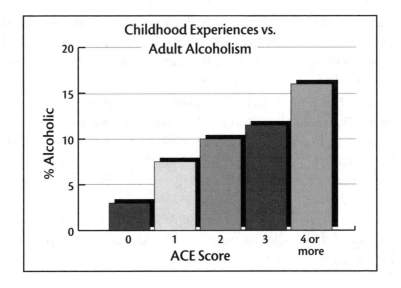

If a person has an ACE score of zero, the individual has almost a 3 percent chance of being an alcoholic. With a score of two, the chance is almost five times higher. With a score of four plus, the chance is 16 percent, and it is seven times as high as someone with zero. The same type of staircase pattern can be seen with smoking.

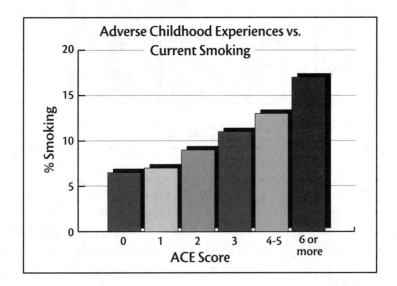

Kaiser has been very interested in why a certain percentage of people do not appear to be helped by their present programs to lose weight or to stop smoking. The hospital system through this research project is thinking more and more that it is related to the family background of the person. Notice that with six or more ACE factors the chance of a person being a smoker is close to one out of five. With zero ACE factors it is close to one out of twenty.

Disasters in the Home

What this is saying loudly is that addiction correlates strongly with an adverse family background. Thin air does not spout out addiction. The soil for it is often prepared by heartache and hurt within the home.

The study also came to another conclusion. Many believe that addiction is an indication of weak character and no spine when, in fact, it has a completely different rationale behind it. The researchers ended up describing these addictive practices as "effective short-term coping devices."* The behaviors are there to kill the pain and give some pleasure. In the context of a truly stressed out home, it makes immense sense. The heart cannot bear pain so it must deal with the disasters in the home. One should not then look at just the behavior, but instead a look should be taken at the pain in the heart.

Obviously Kaiser and the CDC are preoccupied with the medical realities of addiction, and they have isolated the health risk behaviors and the disease conditions that result. Stressed out homes produce these behaviors: smoking, severe obesity, physical inactivity, depression, alcoholism, illicit drug use, injected illegal drug use, and sexual promiscuity. Seven out of the eight (except physical inactivity) are forms of addiction. Disastrously those behaviors set up the person for the following set of diseases: ischemic heart disease, diabetes, stroke, cancer, suicide, skeletal fractures, chronic bronchitis and emphysema, sexually transmitted diseases, and hepatitis.

---

* Felitti lecture.

To say that addictive behavior is unimportant suddenly becomes a silly statement when this progression is examined.

So the heart of the matter is in the home. I remember as I was coming to terms with being raised in an alcoholic home, I reflected on what I knew about my father and grandfather. I thought, from what I was told, my grandfather was a rageoholic, and my father was an alcoholic. That made sense then of what my father had done. He dealt with the pain through drinking, and he had been drinking from his late teens. Then, I asked myself how did that background affect my adult functioning? The answer was workaholism. I carried the same family stress but coped a different way. My way was more socially acceptable. So our generations went from rageaholism to alcoholism to workaholism. Is one better than the other? Interestingly each one of them qualifies as one ACE factor. Workaholism leads to emotional neglect in the family while the other two obviously are stand-alone ACE factors. With the presence of one ACE factor, at least 84 percent of the time there will be at least one more, or several other ACE factors present.

> The challenge is the unaddressed pain. Take away the pain within the home, and people have a chance at life.

Realizing this I have developed a much more sympathetic view of my father. The difficulty is not the alcohol. The challenge is the unaddressed pain. Take away the pain within the home, and people have a chance at life. I was speaking to a friend of mine, Jane. She told me that she discovered by stopping drinking exactly why she was drinking and taking prescription drugs. The pain she had been avoiding was so intense that it almost pushed her back into addiction.

Undercutting Misconceptions

Two dangerous misconceptions challenge what the CDC and Kaiser have found. One simply says, "Addiction is just a matter of chemicals. You take them and you are a goner. Don't take them and everything will be all right." Or a more sophisticated soul might say, "It is just genetics. People are predisposed to be alcoholics, and others are predisposed to sex addiction, and others to heroin. Sure it has everything to do with families, but not with pain within families but what is inherited by families."

The Kaiser study directly addressed that two ways: one by statistics and the other by analysis. The view that the study challenged was, "Addiction is due to the characteristics intrinsic in the molecular structure of some substance."* In simpler terms it is all chemistry. The Kaiser study is a massive challenge to the premise. One must keep underscoring that this ACE study is the largest one in the history of the world (pretty big place and a lot of time). We will return to this shortly, but let's address the genetic argument this way. Genetics or God or evolution (take your pick, I prefer God) has produced a human heart that cannot stand pain, just as the human finger dislikes being in boiling water. Genetics produced the human heart and finger, and genetics produced the rather helpful human aversion to pain! Appealing to genetics as the cause of addiction is just as silly as blaming emotional pain on genetics. Both problems are so common and so huge that they may well have something in common, like one (pain) causes the other (addiction).

One of the more fascinating things about the CDC and Kaiser study is that they were able through statistics to isolate what was the percentage of risk factor directly attributable to an Adverse Childhood Experience. For alcoholism, drug abuse, and IV drug use, they give the "PAR" or Population Attributable Risk. The "PAR" is that percentage of a condition that can be confidently and directly attributed to a cause.

Estimates of the Population-Attributable Risk of ACES for Selected Outcomes in Women

Drug Abuse	**PAR**
Alcoholism	65%
Drug abuse	50%
IV drug use	78%

---

* Felitti lecture.

Notice that for IV drug use the percentage is 78 percent. These percentages are telling us that the environment of the unhealthy home is the nest where addiction is often hatched. So addiction does not fly in the window of the home. In fact, it frequently comes out of the home.

In sum, addiction does not just happen. Often as not it occurs in a context of pain. Addiction is not a matter of genetics: It is part of the constitution of the human soul and body. Addiction is not just chemicals that reach out and grab a person. Because of the pain, it is the person who is doing the grabbing.

Wisdom tells us then that we should look to the harmony of our homes. We should look to the atmosphere that our children are living in. We should look to our own hearts to see whether we are carrying unnecessary pain.

Misunderstanding #3: "I Can't Live Without It"

We have looked at dangerous beliefs that inhabit the culture. These create a false explanation for addiction and lead people to seek for answers in the wrong places. Now we are going to look at the fantasies or dangerous beliefs that lurk in the shadows of people's hearts. Such beliefs pervade the personality and become the soul's identity.

I often have a slightly uncomfortable feeling when speaking with a compulsive or addicted person. I am used to it but it still leaves me with some negative "vibes." That is because I get the feeling when I am talking about the addictive cycle that not a word I am saying is being believed. Instead the man or woman has the following powerful compelling thought grandly supported by instincts: "My heart will not be satisfied with a life without appetite or lust." Or the thought might even be worse than that, "I can't exist without my desires or lusts." Or even worst of all, "All I am is my appetites. I am my addiction."

People absolutely believe those lies! Those untruths become their identity. I watched a man being confronted by his wife, and being begged by his daughter to stop his addiction to pornography. I watched as this same person lost jobs because his employers found Internet pornography stored in immense files on his computer. I spoke with him about how he was more than his addiction, and extended my sympathy. Taking the sympathy and embracing it with tears, he did not change.

What was interesting about this man was that I knew him for 20 years. During that time I did not know about his addiction, but I could not but notice that he was emotionally shut down. He was amiably nice and helpful, but with no affect. No real emotions played across his face and no enthusiasms rushed through his soul. During the conversations, it became obvious that he had the dangerous misunderstanding that all he was, was his sex drive. "All I am is my appetites."

For him, in his instincts, it is absolutely true. There is no existence apart from the appetites dominating his heart. How can that be so? Look at life from his perspective. Growing up in pain, he chose to repress his emotions in the face of the stress that was in the home. Year after year he did this until he became convinced that all that was inside was an empty shell. Nothing was there.

Then came the pleasure of pornography. This pleasure was not dependent upon relationships nor dependent upon his nonexistent emotional life. He could call upon it at anytime. He did not have to relate to his wife; he did not have to deal with her expectations or demands. Also his wife was grossly overweight, and no women in the pictures or the videos had any extra weight on them. In fact, the impenetrable haze of sexuality cushioned him from the demands of life.

Deep in his soul was the belief that he could not exist without sexually stimulating pornography. In one sense he was right. Growing up he had no emotional life and every once in a while he wondered if he existed. If asked to prove that he existed as a person, he would be hard put to prove it. No emotions were in there to solidify his existence within, and no recognizable warm relationships were without to reaffirm the reality of his person. There had been no one on the outside to lovingly describe what they saw in him. He was left with emotional and relational non-existence. The only thing that brought existence or something alive and powerful was lust. Better that than nothing was his belief!

It Doesn't Get Better Than This?

What is such a tragedy is that lust and addiction may be for many the best that life has to offer. I was talking to a young woman, 22 years of age, who was going into Christian ministry. She said she felt that she was ill-prepared for ministry. Not only did she not know much about effectively serving the Lord, she had not come to terms with her family background. She then told me that she was raised in a home with two alcoholic parents. As we talked, I asked her, when she felt someone liked her did it feel like a "drug experience," did it almost make her high? She nodded with surprise. I then asked if she was emotionally shut down. Again she said with surprise, "Yes."

Then, I asked, "Do you sometimes feel that you do not exist? Or it would be hard to prove that you did?" She almost slipped off her chair, and exclaimed she sometimes did. I said that she really needed to address those things, otherwise she was very vulnerable. The irony of the conversation was that she was dedicated to serving the God of heaven and earth and she was walking wounded. She was vulnerable. She needed to address her family background, otherwise she would be very vulnerable to codependency, getting a high off of persons, and addiction. She was already tending to be overweight.

So in a very real sense addiction is a direct continuation of the family background of many. Seen in that light, the ultimate solution is to establish healthy relationships in adult life. Ironically the person from a stressed, abusive, and emotionally shut down background is wide open to dependent emotional relationships. Addiction does not arise out of nowhere.

Misunderstanding #4: "It's Just a Picture on a Screen"

As we have seen in the previous chapter, the temptation, compulsive, addiction cycle is a step into loneliness. That is formally called "disassociation." Naturally such disassociation sets up a person, male or female, to view pornography non-relationally. It would never occur to a male or female to think that the person in the video or picture has a mother too.

The other side of the statement, "It's just a picture on a screen," is "No one is hurt, and you don't have to worry about sexually transmitted diseases." The challenge in all this is to think this through as far as what it says about male–female relationships.

Let's step back and use an illustration that may be helpful. I am a male. I am working in my office, and I have an appointment with a young woman. I have never met her and she wants my advice about something. Arriving for the appointment, she comes into my office and she is a beauty. Also she is not the most modest dresser.

Of course I immediately notice her appearance, and I fixate on it for a second. Then, I have a choice. I can turn the conversation into a pornographic experience or I can turn the conversation into a human one. Having faced that decision thousands of times, I made the choice to turn the conversation into a human experience. If I make the decision to turn the ensuing conversation into a pornographic experience, all I have to do is to refuse to humanize the person I am talking to. My mind will then focus on her appearance and the pleasure it gives, and what's left of my mind will keep the conversation going.

To humanize the conversation, I have to say several things in a very straightforward way to myself. First, "David, this is a human being so talk to who she is, and not to how she appears!" Second, "David, who this person in her heart is massively different than what you see. Discover that person and you will not at all be preoccupied with what you see."

Frankly no great difference exists between an unknown attractive woman walking into an office and an unknown attractive woman appearing in pornography (with the obvious difference of the amount of clothing). But the laden with lust stare from the heart of the male may be essentially the same for each of the two women. The issue is exactly the same: Does the male humanize the woman or as opposed to that, to use the popular term, does he "objectify" her or leave her as an object?

It is not only the men who are doing this to women but more and more women are doing this to men. The majority of credit card purchases made at pornographic sites are made by women. That surprises me but that is what a tape from Focus on the Family said based on what they learned at a pornography convention. In our work in the churches we present the seminar "Addiction Proofing Your Life and Ministry." In it we emphasize that often men are ambushed through their sexuality and women are through the appetite for food. If we do not emphasize though that women are as susceptible as men to sexual addiction, sooner or later we get some pretty angry complaints from women for leaving them out from problems with lust.

So the challenge is for both genders to humanize the other and not to objectify the opposite gender. What are the benefits in doing so? There are three. First, if we treat the other gender relationally we inherently protect ourselves from lust. Sexual compulsion is created by having the heart strip away everything about a person except their sexuality and focus on the visual and sensual. To humanize the person deeply interferes with that process.

Secondly, we humanize ourselves. The more we train ourselves to look beyond the appearance and to look upon the heart, the more human we will become in the process. Thirdly, we will be able to manage our appetites with more and more skill. We will benefit; those about us will benefit; our inner life will benefit.

WHAT CHRISTIANS DON'T KNOW...
CAN ENSLAVE THEM

Purely religious or "Christian" misunderstandings also exist.

Certain prejudices and misinformation seem to be common among religious people.

Misunderstanding #5: "Addiction Is the Worst Possible Sin There Is!"

Particularly if it is sexual sin, many Christians believe that nothing is worse than addiction. This has a twofold effect. First, it permeates the atmosphere of a church or the thinking of religious people and distorts both. Second, it makes the person struggling with addiction feel worse and leads to more isolation and hiding from help.

The actual truth is that addictions and sexual sin are not the worst sins (if a person is interested in such categories). Jesus told a series of stories in Luke 15 to the Pharisees. Jesus wanted them to know about how heaven feels about people. The stories were prompted by the Pharisees' criticism of Jesus for having meals with tax collectors and sinners (or non-observant Jews; they did not keep the Law). In response, Jesus told them the stories of the lost sheep, the lost coin, and the lost son.

In the stories we have a series of descending numbers. In the initial story one sheep out of a hundred is lost. The shepherd leaves the 99 and finds the lost. He is happy about it and he has a celebration. Then, Jesus made the application by saying that heaven rejoices over one sinner who repents as opposed to the righteous who do not need to repent. Following that, Jesus told the story of the lost coin. A woman lost one of ten coins, and she searched diligently for it and was happy when she found it. In the same way heaven rejoices over the sinner who repents, Jesus said.

Finally, he told the story of the prodigal or wasteful son. A father had two sons. The younger one took his inheritance and went to a distant land and wasted it on immoral living. The older brother will later say in the story that he wasted his inheritance on prostitutes. All this time the father did not chase him. Finally the younger son came to his senses after losing all his inheritance and returned to his father. The father was delighted and welcomed his son back. He threw a party, treated the returning son with honor, and prepared special food for the occasion.

The older brother was incensed. He refused to come to the party. The father who did not chase after the younger son *came looking* for the older one. Finding him the father explained that the older brother should be happy because the younger who was dead, so to speak, was now alive again.

This story was directed at the Pharisees, who like the older brother, were not happy. All these younger brothers who were guilty of sin or fornication and such things, to their disgust, were repenting and returning to spiritual life. Jesus invited the younger brothers of this world to change their lives and they were doing so. The point of the story, however, was about the condition of the older brother and the Pharisees. The older brother was in far greater danger because the younger brother's sin was that of the flesh; the older brother's sin was one of the spirit. He considered himself spiritually superior to his younger brother, he was judgmental, and he could find nothing inside himself that was happy with his younger brother's repentance. No love existed in his heart.

The greatest sins we do are not the ones of the flesh. The greatest ones are those of the spirit. *And the greatest sin of all is when we decide that forgiveness, mercy, and grace are something we do not need.* God seemingly does not mind his Son dying for every variety of human sinning, but He appears to have a hard time with those who do not understand grace or forgiveness or their own need of grace.

Many church people seem to have a rough time with people who are addicted and are struggling with sins like pornography, prostitution, and drugs. In one sense, those types of religious people make a lie out of what they profess. Let me explain that this way. Many people in church are theoretical sinners. They have mentally assented to needing a savior, but they have no desperate sense of being failures and wrongdoers. They indeed are theoretical sinners.

For such people Jesus ultimately is a theoretical savior. That is very thin soup indeed!

But many other people have a deep sense of failure, a cringing sense of need, and a hopelessness about themselves. They are real sinners, and for them Jesus is a real Savior. They got into Christianity because no other option existed; they desperately needed help.

We're All Desperate Cases

Many, many times the church is surreal about things like addiction. The conservative churches preach and teach that everyone is a sinner and is destined to hell because of their wretchedness. But when the church leaders stumble across the reality of drug addiction, the enslaving power of pornographic addiction, the slavery of bulimia and anorexia, they send these individuals to everywhere else but the church for help. Those kind of churches appear to be appealing to theoretical sinners who in reality only need a theoretical savior.

Classic Christianity teaches that everyone desperately needs help but in different ways. Yes, the addicted needs help but also the self-satisfied desperately needs more help. As Jesus said, He did not come for the righteous but for the sinner. Also He said that those who are sick need a physician such as Himself, but those that are healthy do not need Him.

> As the Pharisees were observing, they were continually saying to His disciples, "Why is your Teacher continuing to eat with the tax collectors and sinners?" But after Jesus heard, He said, "No need exists for those who are robustly healthy for a physician, but those who are in a bad way. But go and learn what this means: 'I continually desire mercy and not sacrifice,' for I did not come to call the righteous, but sinners" (Matthew 9:11-13).

That is a sarcastic way of saying that the self-satisfied religious can go to hell where they truly belong. No sense of need in a world and life like this is a true mark of great spiritual craziness. Even the best of us are not all that removed from the worst of us.

Pure and robust Christianity views only one act as the great sin, and that is the refusal to accept the God who died for us on the cross. All sin and wrongdoing was dealt with there. To pick and choose among sins is to minimize the damage we really cause one another, and secondly it misunderstands that the Son of God Jesus died for each sin committed on this planet. Therefore, to look down on addiction as a particularly terrible sin is to elevate ourselves falsely, and miss the great implications of Christianity.

Misunderstanding #6: "Addiction Is a Secular Concept"

Some Christians have a suspicious turn of mind. It just seems to go with certain brands of Christianity and certain brands of religion. I do not think Christianity produces suspicious people, but I think people produce suspicious brands of Christianity. So on the face of it when the culture uses such terms as codependency or addiction or compulsion, such Christians become nervous because the words are not in the Bible.

What they forget is that every word in our English Bible is a word translated from the Greek or Hebrew Bible. Furthermore, the Bible has been translated thousands of times for people around the world. It has been translated for the sophisticated Chinese scholar and for the illiterate Indian in a Brazilian jungle. Every time a word in the Hebrew Old Testament or the Greek New Testament is translated, it has to be accommodated to how the recipients understand things and how their language works. Imagine the accommodation taking place for a Brazilian rain-forest Indian when it comes to the words "camel" and "snow."

So sometimes when certain Christians object to words being used, such as addiction, they are not realizing that every religious term they use is actually a monumental accommodation to their culture and language. Let's illustrate this with addiction. Paul the apostle says in Romans 6:16-20 that whatever we are enslaved to is our master and controls us, so that he was grateful that the Roman Christians abandoned their slavery to sin, and enslaved themselves to God. He used the everywhere present institution of slavery to describe how we relate to sin and God. Another way of saying this is that we have to choose our addictions: to our flesh or to God. Instead of the ancient institution, slavery, modern terminology, addiction, could be used in that context.

Or another example is that in Galatians 5:19-21, Paul described what are the works of the flesh (that is the normal translation and it is a consistent and good one). These works are alcoholism, sexual promiscuity, superstition, anger, contentions, and many others. If someone were to ask me, what is a work of the flesh, I would say a relationally destructive addictive behavior. Instantly a contemporary American would get it, and then possibly ask, "Does the Bible address addiction too?" My response would be, "Absolutely!" The contemporary might then say, please show me because I need help. If I said the Bible just addresses works of the flesh and enslaving unethical habits but not addictions, I would be grossly inaccurate, and worse than that I would be totally unhelpful to desperately needy people.

The greatest reason the church and preachers should accommodate the language they use so that they are understood is that God accommodated Himself to us by sending His Son to become one of us. So when a person with a circumscribed view of Christianity says, "Addiction is a secular concept—the Bible calls all of this sin, and that is all we need to understand," the tragedy is twofold: They are very unhelpful and secondly they contradict how the religion they believe in actually works.

Misunderstanding #7: "God Is Too Holy to Be Invited into My Mess"

One religious belief that is not really a Christian truth is another dangerous misunderstanding. It has two variations to it. The first is that God is too holy to tolerate or help the addict or compulsive person. A variation of this same kind of thinking is, "After I clean this up, He will help me."

Again such thinking is a massive misunderstanding about how Christianity works. God loves people (period). His love is not dependent upon how few or how many sins we produce. What He wants to know is whether we will respond to His love or not, not how moral we are. The question of our morality has already been settled: we are not. Therefore, God is willing to work with us as we are, and not as we would like to be. I would like to be a much nobler and better person than I am but I am stuck with who I am. The fact that God is willing to work with me as I am (I do not have to create an illusion of myself) wins my heart, love, and loyalty. Paul said it this way in his letter to Titus:

> Real Christianity *assumes* people are addicted or enslaved to lusts and pleasures... God's intervention in our lives is not based upon our righteous deeds but on our desperate need and His affection for us.

> We also once were continually foolish ourselves, unpersuaded, continually erring, continually enslaved to various lusts and pleasures [a nice way of saying addicted], spending our life in malice and envy, hateful, continually hating one another. But when the kindness of God our Savior and affection for humanity appeared, He saved us, *not on the basis of deeds which we have done in righteousness,* but according to His mercy, by the washing of regeneration and renewing by the Holy Spirit (Titus 3:3-5).

Notice that real Christianity *assumes* people are addicted or enslaved to lusts and pleasures. Note also that God's intervention in our lives is not based upon our righteous deeds but on our desperate need and His affection for us.

This matches what we have seen in chapter 2, where we saw that God does not abandon His own and He works and relates to His own based upon where they are in life, not based on where they would like to be or where He would like us to be. We do not have to become a certain kind of person to merit God's love and help. But we do have to be the kind of person who recognizes personal need and His love and help.

In the coming chapter we shall see how immensely practical God's help is as we examine the topic of the Holy Spirit and addiction. If we sense that we are needy people who are weak, this chapter should be of great encouragement to us. As we struggle with temptation, compulsion, and addiction, someone else needs to be remembered particularly by the Christian. That Someone is the Person of the Holy Spirit.

FIVE

Help from the Best Counselor in the World

At the heart of everything exists a stupendous, wondrous, loving reality. Beautifully pure and wondrously relational, the reality is the Trinity. To express its beauty one must ascend into poetry. This poetry of existence and life, however, often goes unrecognized by many Christians. That is the poetry of our Triune God. Christianity teaches only one God exists but this God continually relates within as Three Persons and to us in the same way. In the Bible they are inseparable, but also are complete Persons who are profoundly united and of one purpose. For example, Jesus spoke of how He would give eternal life to those who believe Him. Then, He went on to say that He and the Father will protect those who do believe.

> My Father, who has given them to Me, is greater than all; and no one is able to seize them out of the Father's hand. I and the Father are one thing (John 10:29-30).

Notice how He first emphasized the unity of purpose of His Father and Himself: They are going to protect their own. Then, He went from the unity of purpose to the unity of their nature. They are one thing. Being one thing means among other realities that they cannot exist apart from one another. For the Trinity to be the One, there has to be the two Others. The Three are the Father, Son, and the Holy Spirit. Examples of their interconnected unity abound in the Bible. The Great Commission underscored their unity by attaching each Person to the singular word Name:

> After having gone therefore make disciples of all the nations, immersing them in the name [authority, reputation, and works] of the Father and the Son and the Holy Spirit (Matthew 28:19).

Again note that the word "name" is in the singular and three Persons are attached to it. That reflected the unity of nature and purpose in love that our Triune God has. When one speaks of Jesus Christ, the Son of God, another thought always has to be joined to it, and that is, How does the Father and the Holy Spirit relate? Never in the Bible are the other two members of the Trinity an afterthought. For one to be present the other two have to be active never passive.

So as we address temptation and compulsion and addiction, we have spoken of the Person and role of the Son and Father. Each member of the Trinity is involved with our deliverance from addiction. The Father is the One we associate with. The Son gives us an infinitely positive identity instead of the history we have of sin and failure. The Holy Spirit, moreover, is present and ready and willing to help us at our point of greatest weakness. As we saw in chapter 2, God has sent the Spirit specifically to deal with addiction. In this present chapter we shall see that wherever we have a struggle, we have a great reason for courage and activity.

The Role of the Spirit of God

We can list the ministry of the Spirit in the following way:

ORGANIZE YOUR LIFE AROUND THE SPIRIT!
(GALATIANS 5:16)

▼

FOLLOW THE "TUGS" OF THE SPIRIT! (5:18)

▼

BE INFLUENCED BY THE FRUIT, OR CHARACTER,
OF THE SPIRIT! (5:22)

▼

TAKE THE INDIVIDUAL STEP BY THE SPIRIT! (5:25)

As we look at these different elements, certain conclusions are clear. First, the Holy Spirit wants to influence the entirety of our lives. Second, He is an active presence in the Christian's life whether the Christian acknowledges that or notices that. Third, He wants to produce character in our lives, an atmosphere of loving, joyful tranquility wherein we become other-centered people. Lastly, to do this we must be sure that when we face a crossroads, we walk down the road with the Spirit.

But the most important reality for the person who is struggling with temptation, compulsion, and addiction is that the Spirit is within us, and is waiting at the place of our next temptation.

Let's take apart these realities. In chapter 5 of the letter to the Galatians, Paul has spoken of the works of the flesh, which we have understood as referring to compulsive and addictive behaviors. It was also in this chapter where Paul told us that the flesh has two weapons it uses against us: strong negative emotions (moods), and lusts or appetites. But it was also in this chapter Paul spoke of the role of the Spirit of God in deliverance. It appears that He is the Person who is within us of the Trinity designated to deal with addiction and emotional pain.

The argument in the letter to the Galatian Christians revolved around the use of Law and the customs of Judaism within this new religion of Christianity that those from Galatia (now western Turkey) had embraced. Essentially Paul said to them that Law and the customs had no place in biblical Christianity because a great new force had entered the lives of believers. That great new force was the transcendent Persons of the Trinity, particularly the Person of the Holy Spirit. Since the Holy Spirit is deity, He does not need the rules of the Law or the customs of Judaism to help Him out as He helps us out.

Paul told the Christians that they were freed from those things, so that they should feel no obligation. But they should not take advantage of this freedom selfishly but instead they should allow the Holy Spirit to do His work in their lives.

A New Way to Organize Life

As an alternative to the past sinful lives and the present temptation to be preoccupied with rules, Paul told them to cooperate with the Spirit.

> I am continually saying, be *organizing your life* around the quality of the Spirit, and you will absolutely not bring a desire of the flesh to completion (Galatians 5:16).

Many translations say "walk," but something more than a stroll is meant. The form of the word means "walking around through life"; it is emphasizing the Christian's path through existence or life. As the Christian does that, and enters a new area of life or experience in life or a new relationship in life, that part should be brought into harmony with the Spirit or the qualities of the Spirit.

Often all of us enter a new area or part of life or relationship where we run on habits and our habits get us into trouble. I can remember when I was bitterly disappointed by friends whom I had known for a decade. I sulked and felt morose and sad. It took me about three months to come to terms with the disappointment, pray about it realistically, and come to a place of peace. I believe that peace was a direct work of the Spirit of God. And so for that disappointment I had come to arrange my life around qualities from the Spirit, peace and love.

If different areas of life are brought under the influence of the

Spirit of God, the promise was given that a lust or appetite would not be brought to completion. What it is certainly saying is that the Christian will experience the appetite from the flesh, but it will not work its way out to dominate the life. Instead the fruit of the Spirit with its love, joy, and peace will dominate.

The reality is that there are many places in life where we come to a crossroads. We can either succumb to stress and look to our appetites for relief and pleasure or we can turn to God the Father, share our lives with Him, and find relief and tranquility through the Spirit of God.

The Spirit Is Already There

In the next verse Paul told his audience that in our lives the flesh with its appetites and moods are in opposition to the working of the Spirit of God. These are in a natural opposition because each has a different goal for our life. The flesh wants our lives to be dominated by pleasure, but the Spirit wants our lives dominated by the kind of character that Jesus Christ has.

Then, something of fundamental importance is said: "These are set in opposition to one another, so that you will not do those things you would (Galatians 5:17)." Wherever the flesh wants to lead us, the Spirit is already there! The Holy Spirit places Himself at each point of weakness and temptation. It does not matter if it is the Christian who has completely succumbed to addiction or a mature healthy Christian who is being tempted, the Spirit is there at the point of weakness to help.

During the American Civil War, the Northern army would frequently invade the South to attack Richmond, the capital of the Confederacy. Every time the armies would surge towards Richmond, General Lee and his army would meet them and usually defeat them. The process became downright predictable. In the same way, the invasions of the flesh into our hearts will have the awaiting Holy

Spirit. Not only is the Holy Spirit awaiting the attacks of the flesh, the Holy Spirit is also waiting on us to cooperate with Him.

Imagine the power that is made available to us. Ultimately the flesh is a mindless urge enveloped in an atmosphere of discomfort and pushy emotions. Its opponent is a Divine Person with omnipotence, infinite power at His disposal. To take advantage of this powerful Person is wisdom indeed.

The result of the Spirit's work is that we will not be able to do the things that we would, that the flesh would want us to do. Again this does not mean that we will not sense the pull of temptation nor the force of uncomfortable emotions. But it does mean we have a way to turn and a Person will meet us as we turn.

The "Tugging" of the Spirit

Paul assumed that the Spirit is a very active agent in the life of the believer. For He went on to say,

> Since by the qualities from the Spirit you are being led or prompted, you are not at all under law (Galatians 5:17).

What this is saying is that a partnership has been created for us by God the Father with the Holy Spirit. We are expected to take areas of life into the Father's presence to sort them out. As we do so the Spirit of God will be ministering to us.

Immediately someone reading this will think and maybe even say, "Certainly I feel the impact of the flesh in my life, it's very powerful, but I am not sure at all that I feel or sense the prompting of the Spirit of God." What that person needs to remember is that the flesh is a "mugger." It just comes and starts beating us up. A beating is hard to miss. On the other hand, the Spirit is a "tugger." We may be so overwhelmed with the mugging that we miss the tugging.

Also we have to understand the two different goals that the flesh and the Spirit have. The flesh's goal is to enslave us; the goal of the Spirit is to teach us our freedom in Christ. Unfortunately Christians who are used to the enslaving power of the flesh, and the demands of false religious performance, may find the whole idea of freely participating in God's life as foreign, foreboding, and somehow totally unrealistic with where they are in life. Yet that is the Spirit's goal, freedom. As Galatians 5:1 said, "It was for freedom that Christ set us free."

Further, some of the "tuggings" of the Spirit may be ridiculously simple, such as prompting us to pray instead of focusing on a desire, or to read the Bible instead of sexually fantasizing, or to talk to a friend instead of isolating oneself. These promptings have to come softly so that we can partner with the Spirit and participate intelligently. Possibly some may want the Spirit to show up with a bullhorn and an electric cattle prod. It won't happen, because that is how the devil and the flesh do things but not God the Father.

Paul went on to tell the Galatians how the flesh does indeed do things. He wrote that the works or habits of the flesh were self-evident. Those habits manifested themselves in the sexual area by acts of sexual immorality, by habits of mind that were sexually compulsive, and by intense licentiousness (Galatians 5:19). Obviously these things are found throughout sexual addiction. Then, in the next verse he addressed false religious practice. Paul said idolatry and sorcery or the misuse of drugs in religion and magical practices were also promoted by the flesh.

Then, he gave a weighty list of that which afflicts relationships: "enmities, strife, jealousy or zeal, angry outbursts, contentions, dissensions, factions" (Galatians 5:21). What Paul appears to be saying is that it is not people who necessarily poison relationships, but it is the angry push of the flesh that spits out the venom that so hurts people. When we are angry we are focused on other persons, but what we need to notice is the intensity of the emotions and desires that are there. They are an entirely different problem and challenge than the possibly hurtful people we are dealing with. In the coming chapter it will become very important to be able to isolate the emotions we feel about others and come to spiritual terms with them. Oftentimes people caught up with carnality, the impact of the flesh on their lives, are preoccupied with people and really do not notice their emotional state. We cannot do anything about what we cannot see or refuse to see. Paul told the Galatian Christians that those emotional states and maddening desires were the problem. In the next chapter we will speak of that in detail, so that we can see how to manage and change those emotions.

In contrast Paul went on to share the emotional states and desires that the Spirit wants to produce are driven by love, joy, and peace. Paul had such confidence in the presence of the Holy Spirit and the emotional states and desires that the Spirit could produce that he said the impact will lead the Christian to transcend the law. Literally what Paul was saying is that there was not a law anywhere that would be against loving, happy people.

Many times in Galatians Paul stated the Christian was not under the Law (2:16,19,21; 3:2,5; 3:21). In chapter 5, he stated that it is the presence of the Spirit and His fruit that made the Law unnecessary. Such a marvelous truth has to be understood in the entire context of the Bible. The Law was a major feature of Old Testament truth, and the subject of much New Testament revelation. So for the Law to be set aside in favor of the Person of the Holy Spirit is truly a marvelous and important reality. The liberator has come and we must partner with Him!

The Spirit Is Our Partner Against the Flesh

Paul, then, as he came to the end of chapter 5 of Galatians underscored the two great weapons of the flesh, negative moods (passions) and strong desires. With particularly strong language he stated that the individual who belonged to Christ has killed or crucified the flesh with its two accomplices (2:24).

Now for many believers this verse is confusing. They will feel that it seems more likely the Spirit has been crucified with love and joy, and the flesh is on a rampage. Can Paul be ignoring that reality? That most realistic of men was certainly not. Instead he was just reemphasizing the basic truths of Christianity.

First of all, those who believe the gospel belong to Christ (Galatians 5:24). They gain God as a Father (John 1:12), and they are also sealed with the Person of the Holy Spirit that was promised (Ephesians 1:14). They now are under grace. As a result, the flesh as a system of death and destruction and control has been killed—executed. We are no longer under it.

What is fascinating about 5:24, it states that God did not do that, but we did. Somehow or other we killed the flesh. I think we naturally turn the verse into saying that God crucified the flesh, but it very clearly states that we did it. How could that be? It was actually quite easy. We believed the gospel and the entire system of the flesh was killed. Such was accomplished with probably a very small amount of faith in the face of great doubt. But when the faith was exercised, the flesh was killed.

I think Paul may have phrased it that way because first, it was true, and second, it underscored how important it was to keep exercising faith when it came to temptations of the flesh. It is not self-effort that will free us from the flesh but to respond to the Spirit's prompting to exercise faith. As Paul wrote in Colossians,

> As you therefore have received Christ Jesus the Lord, so walk in Him (Colossians 2:6).

The principle of faith that brought us salvation is also the principle that we must use with reference to the flesh. We can encourage ourselves with the reality that the Holy Spirit is a partner with us to produce that faith (Galatians 5:22).

The image that springs to my mind is that the believer who has crucified the flesh by his exercise of faith in Christ must not then return to the cross where the flesh is hanging quite dead…and revive it. Instead we are called to use the same realities that got us into Christianity, a living relationship with God through faith.

Taking Every Step with the Spirit

Finally, Paul returned to how he started in Galatians 5:16. He encouraged the believers to take the next individual step by the qualities from the Spirit of God.

Since we live by qualities from the Spirit, let us take the next individual step by a quality from the Spirit (Galatians 5:25).

In Galatians 5:16 Paul stated that Christians should arrange each area of their life around the ministry of the Spirit, and in 5:25 he used a different Greek word for walk which meant "to take an individual step." What he was doing was to work through the ministry of the Spirit of God to the believer. The Galatian believer whose native language was Greek would have immediately caught the distinction that Paul was making. This distinction said in effect, "May the entirety of your life and the individual part of your life be under the influence of the Spirit of God."

Time after time I have been surprised how powerful the Spirit is when I take my struggles to God the Father and sort them out with Him. In His presence, as I trust Him and am transparent with Him, tremendous psychological and relational shifts take place. Turmoil turns to tranquility and sorrow to joy. We have not been abandoned. The Spirit is with us.

As we have progressed along we have talked about the nature of addiction, compulsion, and temptation, and we have just looked at what God has provided for us in the Person of the Holy Spirit. We have seen that addiction arises under certain conditions and can be sustained by dangerous misunderstandings. We have underscored the spiritual realities: We have a Father in heaven, we have a Savior who has died for the wrongdoing of addiction, and we have the personal presence of the Spirit of God. Now we are going to see what we have to do to really cooperate with God in dealing with the challenge of addiction. Since we have laid this foundation, now let's get to work, and beat addiction and compulsion!

PART TWO

STRATEGICALLY BEATING
ADDICTION

SIX

Taking Apart the Lifestyle

Living a healthy life for a Christian is a partnership with the divine. It is a partnership in a special sense. We have been made in the image of God as physical beings and with that we have been given the gift of relationship and choice. Also when we become Christians, one of the purposes of God is that we should learn how to use the freedom Christ provides to be other-directed, to be loving. In the writings of Paul we are given the Christian way of self-management of our emotional life including our appetites. Managing the appetites and inner life has a greater goal than becoming merely happy which is a good thing. The better thing God has in mind is to become like Christ.

Indeed this is a partnership with the Trinity. In the previous chapters we have seen that God the Father never abandons His own and that He is willing to adopt and help anyone who comes to Him through Christ. We have also seen that the Holy Spirit is waiting at our point of weakness to help us. Further, through Christ we have the righteousness of God in Him. We have been granted a righteousness that allows us to relax about our guilt and wrongdoing. Instead of running on guilt, we can now run to our Father for help.

But none of those relationships tell us what we are supposed to do. Those relationships tell us what God is doing and intends to do for us. But we need to know and do those things that liberate us from the temptation, compulsion, addiction cycle. That cycle has five parts to it, as we have seen.

PAIN (NEGATIVE MOODS)

▼

DISASSOCIATION

▼

FANTASY WORLD

▼

INITIAL ACT

▼

ACTING OUT

Simply put when a person feels discomfort emotionally, the first thing he or she does is to isolate from people. That is disassociation as we have previously said. Then, the person enters a fantasy world of false pictures, false beliefs, and dangerous misunderstandings that justifies behavior that is self-destructive and relationally damaging. Then, a very robotic first step is taken to directly get pleasure. For example, the first step may be something as simple as turning on a computer for Internet pornography, or taking a walk so as to buy some drug. Then, the last step is to consummate the experience. That brings relief until pain resurfaces and starts the whole cycle over again. As we can see from the chart the fantasy world is in the middle, and is the crucial center for the whole process. The false beliefs of the fantasy world keep the person who is pursuing pleasure from running away from the whole damaging disaster.

Dealing with the Fantasy World

We have been looking at the writings of Paul the apostle, a messenger of Christ in the early church, to see what he had to say about addiction. Romans and Galatians are books we have already looked at. Now we are going to turn our attention to the Letter to the Colossian church. In that book Paul gave a description of the healthy spiritual life. As one looks closely, it almost appears that Paul wrote what he did to deal with the addictive cycle. As a matter of fact, he did—for no great difference exists between the human heart of 2000 years ago and today. The clothing we wear may be different, but the appetites are the same. Indeed the pain levels are similar and temptation works exactly the same way. Paul's approach was spectacularly successful in its time, and it should be just as successful today.

The reason for such confidence is that, as we will soon see, Paul anticipated (I do not think he did this consciously) the addictive cycle. Each part of his description of our spiritual partnership with God the Father addressed a distinct aspect of the cycle. So we will turn our attention to what he wrote to the Colossians. What we will find is all five of the elements of the cycle were addressed, but in a different order. Paul will actually start with the one that I have said is most important, the fantasy world.

"Just Do It" Doesn't Do It

But before we plunge into his open assault on the fantasy world, we should examine how he started that assault. Paul wanted to make it crystal clear what he believed did not work. He wanted us to understand that rules do not work!

> Since all of you have died with Christ to the basic principles of the world, why as if living in the world, do you allow yourself to be ordered about, such as, "Do not handle! Do not taste! Do not touch!" (Colossians 2:20-21).

The human heart loves rules for rules' sake. The mysterious allure of rules is its subtle compliment to our ego. To be given a rule means that whoever the rule giver is, that one actually expects that we can keep them. Implicit in any rule is a pat on the back saying, "You can do this!"

God did not pay us such a compliment. We cannot do rules. Rules do not work because the human heart is unimaginably weak.

> Paul's approach was spectacularly successful in its time, and it should be just as successful today.

Paul believed that if people could be moral and good based upon rules, then Christ died needlessly (Galatians 2:21). Paul believed something deeply different than the lazy righteousness of the rule givers and keepers. He believed that morality and character were the fruit of a life process that did not start with rules but started at a far different place. That place was where pride was abandoned: We cannot be moral; we cannot keep the rules; we are fully incapable of being good. Paul started his point of moral change at a much different point than optimistic moralism (a belief that keeping the rules is the sole duty of being human). But before he got to that point, he wanted to make sure that it was clearly understood that rules—negative rules that said repeatedly, "Do not!"—do not work.

In the verse following 2:21-22, Paul went on to say that these rules normally dealt with things that perish with their use. Food, for example, when consumed was gone. Therefore, those rules did not address significant realities like relationships and the existence of God. Those rules were preoccupied with things that ultimately had no great significance. Paul recommended a spirituality dealing with the great issues, God and relationships.

Superficially rules have an attraction because many believe that morality can only be achieved by a "white-knuckle" approach. The more discomfort and pain we experience the better person we should be. Paul went on in Colossians to describe religious "white-knuckling":

These are matters which have, to be sure, the appearance of wisdom in "will-worship," and humiliation, and severe treatment of the body, but certainly of no value against the pleasure-seeking desires of the flesh (Colossians 2:23).

Morality as weight lifting was what Paul was describing. I become more moral if I work out constantly, discipline myself, discomfort myself, and demand of my will what God Himself does not demand—which is character. The Christian assumption is that life does not work that way. Character does not flow out of will, nor out of effort, nor out of self-inflicted pain. Character flows out of deeper streams. Character flows out of the deep instinctive picture that we have of ourselves. Character flows out of a mysterious union with the different realities that Paul described, Jesus taught, and the early church promoted. Character starts with how we intuitively see ourselves. That intuitive picture controls who we are.

The Power of Identity

One of the several things that our nonprofit ministry does is to teach people about the influence of family and cultural backgrounds on their lives. What we continually say is that "instinct will always trump information." When instinct and information are face to face and competing, instinct wins.

Instincts are very powerful. My wife has a fear of spiders that she has passed on to our daughter. I could lecture my wife on the different variety of spiders in this world. I could bring out a manual and share how very few of them are poisonous and dangerous. I could tell her that scientists estimate that several times a year while we are sleeping we actually swallow those creatures whole as they are wandering about! And we survive that very well! But when Carol goes into the bathroom and sees one, I am certain the next thing I will hear is a loud frightened yell saying, "David, please come quick and kill the spider." Always she will be standing outside the bathroom until the deed is done. Her instincts will always trump my advice and information.

Family Influence

As we work with people to help them see how powerful family background influence is, we will often divide them up in groups by family background. Just after Christmas we were working with a Campus Crusade conference, and we were lecturing on family backgrounds. We gave them a simple questionnaire of 15 questions to fill out. Based on adding up their yes and no answers, we divided them up into three family backgrounds: healthy, confused, and stressed or dysfunctional.*

We had 85 in the healthy background group, 88 in the confused family background group, and 155 in the dysfunctional family background group. To show the influence of instinct over information, I interviewed the different groups. I asked the students from a healthy family background to raise their hands if they could trust people easily. Eighty-plus hands went up. I went over to those from a dysfunctional family and asked how many found it easy to trust people, and only eight hands went up!

Then, I interviewed several individual students from the healthy group, and three of them volunteered what I personally was surprised at. They said that they had believed up to that exercise that everybody came out of families like theirs, happy, stable, trusting, affectionate families. Three in a row said that. These are 18- to 19-year-old university students at secular schools. I could hardly believe my ears. Then, I interviewed an eloquent young woman from the dysfunctional group and she said what I had an easier time believing.

"I don't believe such people exist," she said flatly as she looked over at the students from healthy homes.

"Do you think that they are telling the truth?" I asked her.

---

* To learn more about this, see my book *Becoming Who God Intended*, chapter 6. The questionnaire is in the back of the book.

"No, they can't be. There can't be homes like that."

What was being said and observed was a shock to both groups. Their instincts had such a firm grip over their view of reality that they could not believe what the large group across from them was saying.

What they were showing displayed the power of instinct, but more exact than that the power of identity. Identity is that picture we have of ourselves that has been painted across our hearts by our parents, our life experiences, and our culture. This picture determines how I view myself, the world, and God. The Bible and Paul the apostle believe that identity is one of the great powerful forces in this world.

Let me take a more bizarre example. I suspect that when you get up in the morning, if you are married, you have no problem deciding what side of the closet you are going to pick your clothes from. If you are female, you will pick female clothes to wear that day. If you are male, you will pick male clothes. Why do you do this? Because you have the assumption that you are male or female.

But for some people, the choice is not so easy. Some believe that they are men trapped in women's bodies or they are women trapped in men's bodies. How they got that belief we are not concerned with (although I think I have some pretty good guesses). Their bodies do not match their instinctive belief. It does not matter how much evidence we give, nor does the evidence of their own anatomy matter. What they instinctively believe trumps everything. Reality as we know it has no impact on them.

Harnessing the Power

What Paul in Colossians wanted to do was to harness the power of identity to address the challenge of addiction and to also challenge the fantasy world. Strategically he recognized that the great enemy was that false world. Deal with that and the war was well on its way to being won. Our instincts are what drive our relationships, our decisions, and our habits. Change the instincts by changing our pictures of reality, and we will have a profound inner renewal.

Going back to Campus Crusade, one of the students, Kathy, gave me a huge smile at the winter conference. She was in the conference office behind the counter, and she flashed me an enthusiastic grin. I had to think for a few hours about who she was and then I remembered. Eighteen months before she had gone through the Family Background exercise at a conference in San Diego. Initially she was left in a state of sadness at what she learned about her family background. At the same time she learned at that conference that she had a "Dad" in heaven who enjoyed her, liked her, valued her, and adored her. She started believing that, and then a year ago she went through the exercise again at a winter conference. Kathy was one of the students I interviewed. I asked her if the exercise last June was helpful to her. She loved it and said it rocked her world. I then asked what was the most valuable thing about the exercise.

"It was what I also learned at that time, that I have a Father in heaven who likes me and I can trust. I have a Dad in heaven who is happy with me."

She then broke down weeping as the young ladies around her placed their arms about her. She had transitioned from the instincts of her family background to the instincts of the new family of God. That was easy to tell because her emotions were enslaved to her new set of instincts and therefore she wept. Her identity had changed from a devalued woman to a highly prized child of God.

New Instincts

That is what Paul the apostle wanted to happen in the lives of the Christians he was writing to. He wanted them to see themselves in a different way. He wanted them to develop a new set of Christian family instincts.

First, Paul wanted them to understand that they had a new family history before God. Our families have created an experience and history having a massive impact on us. Now Paul gave the Christians an entirely new family history. He alluded to that in Colossians 2:20:

> Since you died with Christ to the basic principles of this world…

Paul and the New Testament assumed when a person became a Christian, the individual was given a new family history.

Our two children are adopted. I will never forget the two times we had to appear before a judge to sign the papers to make them legally and completely our own. Carol and I had to agree that our new children had all the rights and privileges of any biologically born child. We were happy to do that. We also had to agree in writing that to withhold financial and parental care was illegal and would open us up to criminal prosecution. One thing that we did not agree to but would naturally happen is that our two children who were babies when we adopted them would also inherit the family history and traditions.

Of necessity they inherited my relatives (both normal and strange ones), Carol's relatives (both normal and strange), and also both of our family histories. They became linked to my family history of growing up in Buffalo, New York, and Carol's history of growing up in Pennsylvania. They inherited both present family relationships and past family disasters, triumphs, tragedies, and also some mediocre memories.

Should God do any less for those who trust in His Son? He does not. He shares the family history with us. That family history is the critical central events of the earthly history of Christ. Those central events are the crucifixion, suffering, death, resurrection, ascension and session (being seated on God's throne in heaven), and reign.

All family members everywhere exist within the history and relationships of their family. So indeed, Christians are participants in the family history of God. Except God the Father went a dramatic step further. Instead of just being family members who have a wonderful brother in the family named Jesus who has suffered, died, and was resurrected, Christians are counted from the Father's perspective to have participated in those events with Jesus.

With God Christians are not the sum total of their sins, failures, and shame. We are the sum total of what Jesus has done for us. From the Father's viewpoint a fourth cross was at Golgotha and we were on it. We suffered and died on that cross. When Christ was laid on a limestone slab in the tomb, we were placed on a nearby slab in the tomb. When Jesus walked out of the graveyard, we walked out of that graveyard with Him. As He ascended to heaven, we were there with Him. Now that He is seated on the Father's throne in heaven, we are seated next to Him. His arm is around us.

Physically and emotionally we experienced nothing of this. As adopted daughters and sons of God, Christ's central history is counted to be our own from the Father's perspective. That is why Paul wrote the words we looked at on the previous page:

> Since all of you have died with Christ to the basic principles of the world…(Colossians 2:20).

New Pictures

That new history is how the Trinity sees it, and that is how we should see it. Paul told the Christians in Colossae that in relationship to God they had a radically different means of approach to the issue of dealing with the flesh. Instead of building a fantasy world of self-serving appetite revolving around falsehood, the Christian can build her or his approach to appetites on a totally different premise—we are accepted in Christ. The person who is struggling with temptation, compulsion, and addiction builds life around desires, memories of failure and defeat, and "video clips" of previous experiences of giving into pleasure. The matrix is deadly: Desires drive the person's imagination into a slavery of constantly playing video clips of pleasure from the past in anticipation of the pleasure shortly to come. Then, the individual defines himself or herself by that experience.

Unnoticed is the massive passivity of the enslaved person's imagination. The imagination is a pathetic, unwilling slave to the desires. Never noticed is the amazingly passive imagination. What is in the imagination drives them, but they do not drive or manage their imagination. *The tool to deal with identity and instinct is the imagination.* That is why Paul addressed it without ever mentioning the word. One very important fact to file away is that in our culture the imagination means to perceive that which is untrue or false or nonexistent. In Christianity we use the imagination, an incredibly powerful force, to view the world, God, and ourselves how the Trinity sees things.

Paul, then, in Colossians 3, directly addressed what the Christians in the church should be putting into their imagination and what that perception will permit them to do.

> Since then, all of you have been raised (from the dead) with Christ, seek the things (the relationships) above, where Christ is being seated to the right of God. The relationships above, all of you set your perspective around, not the things (the rules) upon the earth. For all of you have died, and your *life principle* has been deeply hidden with Christ in relationship to God (Colossians 3:1-3).

Paul called the believers to presume and picture how God sees them: suffering, dying, and being raised with Christ. To grapple with this they would have used their imaginations. As they picture themselves being raised with Christ, two dynamic things would happen. First, as they used their imaginations to do that their emotions would naturally match the reality. Indeed the Spirit of God would give them a "hypercharge" of emotion as they saw themselves coming out of the tomb with Jesus. Second, they would start reclaiming their imagination for its God-intended mission of seeing reality the way God does. This way of seeing ourselves is called the "life principle" in the third verse. Such a way of living is known to the members of the Trinity and is revealed to us. This life principle will eventually be revealed when Christ returns, but now it has to be entered into by faith.

Our Association with the Father

Paul started His assault on the addictive cycle with the fantasy world with its domination of the imagination. He went on to address disassociation, stepping into isolation, and loneliness. His answer to disassociation was to associate with God the Father.

In this he contrasted two things. He contrasted the rules of chapter 2, "Touch not, taste not, handle not!" with the relationships created by our union with Christ. The first set of things, Paul called the things on the earth, and the second set of things, he called the things in the heavens. Certainly the things in the heavens are not another set of rules, instead they are the relationships created by our union with Christ.

We can associate with God the Father based on being accepted with Christ. Many Christians unfortunately base their relationship with God on accepting the gospel and then on their follow-up or subsequent performance. If they do well, they feel good, and then they freely talk to God. In true Christianity, talking with the Father is based on what Christ has done for us and not what we have done for God.

Dealing with Negative Moods

In the addictive cycle the first element is unaddressed pain or negative moods in the life. That discomfort is what drives the entire cycle. What is fascinating was that Paul placed dealing with discomfort and emotional pain third. He first established the reason for a transparent relationship with God, our union with Christ. Then, on the basis of that union, we are to relate to the Father. As we relate to the Father, Paul told us to do the following:

> You immediately put to death, therefore, your members which are upon the earth, with regards to sexual immorality, sexual uncleanness, negative mood, wrong desire, and greed which is idolatry (Colossians 3:5).

Notice the "therefore" carefully. That presumed the two previous principles are being heeded: to accept that we have been raised with Christ, and to relate to the Father, putting our perspective on heavenly relationships. We cannot put to death these very strong appetites without the previous two being practiced.

The order was to put to death these appetites, that is rid ourselves of the effects, the force, and the control of those wrong desires. Paul was assuming something revolutionary. We can in partnership with God totally nullify the pull of these appetites. We cannot do this once for all time, but when we are under their assault we can. The next day they may return. But the next day we have a way to deal with them again.

As we remain in the Father's presence in heaven, and wrong moods and desires strike, we can sort them out. This assumption of staying in the Father's heavenly presence is underscored by an odd-sounding phrase that Paul used: "Put to death, therefore, your members upon the earth." Paul presumed that the believer, in effect, existed in heaven in union with Christ. But their bodily members were located on the earth!

Paul said the believers could reduce controlling sexual urges to memories; alter negative moods so as to transition them to love, joy, and peace; and reduce greed to a thought instead of having it as a controlling "god."

So from their position and perspective in heaven, the believers were to deal with what was afflicting their bodily members, and kill it.

Paul said the believers could reduce controlling sexual urges to memories; alter negative moods so as to transition them to love, joy, and peace; and reduce greed to a thought instead of having it as a controlling "god." These nasty feelings are not the kinds of things we would tell others about. Normally we don't tell those about us that we are driven by greed and consumed by sex and dominated by desperate and needy emotions. But these are the things that dwell deep in the heart.

This is quite surprising from a modern contemporary perspective that such control is possible. Psychologists would very much hesitate to say that their counselees could be given such control. Medical doctors with their pills would not even attempt to address all the emotional issues Paul talked about. It would take the help of God Himself to produce such results.

Paul in this third step addressed those feelings and desires that were deep within. In a real sense, the arena he addressed was the private personal world that we will hardly share with anyone. But Paul sought integration on the deepest level and he revealed how Christianity did that. Taking advantage of the radical acceptance in Christ, Paul shared how these things should be worked out with God the Father.

An Example of Dissipation

Jim was fixated on Judy, a woman at work. He sexually fantasized about her several times a day. All through the day at work he was experiencing low-level lust because of his preoccupation. Jim was married and was a Christian. Finally it struck him that what he was experiencing was not right. Sensing a soft prompting (which he later figured out was from the Spirit of God), he decided he would tell God the Father about it.

He knew enough about the Bible to realize that telling the blunt truth to God was a permissible thing to do. "Father, I am lusting all the time after Judy and I hardly recognize that my wife Sue exists," he said to God. He went so far as to describe his sexual fantasies. As he did so he noticed that the impact of the images and the desires was lessening. After several more minutes, he stopped praying and went back to what he was doing.

Several hours later he returned to prayer, and a powerful thought struck him and it was a question. "Who is your God? Judy and your lust for her or the Father?" was the forceful question that gripped his heart. He then realized that God and Sue had been pushed aside by his lust. Then, he asked himself a searching question: "Can I trust myself to God that if I share my lusts with God that everything will work out all right, and I'll be happy?" He decided that he would choose the Father as his God and not his lust, and in addition he would trust God the Father with his well-being and his future.

Significant peace entered him. He felt that the sexual pressure was dissipating rapidly. He was feeling released. He did what Paul talked about in Colossians 3 and it worked. There was nothing mechanical in the process. The conversation in God's presence was brutally transparent and honest. God honored the conversation. Deep inner change started.

Dealing with Painful Relationships

What Paul described were the sensations and desires deep within. After sharing how important it was to deal with them, the apostle went on to another source of pain, relationships with people.

> Even now all of you immediately take off [like clothing] all of the following: anger, angry outrage, malicious feelings, slander, shameful speech from your mouth. Stop lying to each other after having discarded the old worn out man [identity] with its habits, and after putting on the new one, the one being qualitatively renewed unto a personal knowledge according to the Image of its Creator (Colossians 3:8-10).

What these verses were describing was relationships that have gone to seed. Bitterness has set in and all the person was is angry outrage. These were the emotions of failed relationships. What happened in the midst of failed relationships was that lying became acceptable. The assumption was that the other person certainly did not deserve being told the truth.

In the ocean the warm water flows like a river over the cold water down under. Paul was now describing what was hotly visible on the surface. To communicate that Paul used the image of clothing. Clothing was what people saw, and Paul described what people saw coming off the angry, bitter person.

Below that were the feelings of lust, and loss and inadequacy (the strong negative moods), and greed. In the order that Paul gave, the Christian first killed off those deeper emotions that certainly were the launching pad for those relationally angry responses. If those deeper emotions were replaced by love, joy, and peace, then the relational emotions could be dealt with.

Jim had come to terms with his lust for Judy. He felt peace and more and more serenity. He could be around Judy and not be preoccupied with unacceptable fantasies. He saw her more and more as a real person and not just a "sensation generator." Also Jim noticed that he was more peaceful, joyful, and honestly loving. Also he saw that he had been withholding his affection from his wife Sue, and he was also holding grudges against her. Those grudges created the excuses that his conscience needed to permit him to be preoccupied with Judy. Since he had come to terms with his lust and sense of need and lack, he found that he could address his relationship with his wife in a healthy way. He felt free to reinvest in her, and to share his frustrations with her in a more tender way. As he did so, he felt renewed affection and sexual attraction for Sue. Jim was really struck by how much more freedom he had to emotionally invest in his wife. The addictive allure he had for Judy was broken. Freedom came to enjoy and love his wife. Deep healing had taken place and now he was free to relate in a healthy way.

Paul described two different sets of emotions and desires: One set dealt with the deep world of need and lack (sexuality, deprivation, and greed), and the other set dealt with exploded relationships. The first set preoccupied the person with what he or she needed or wanted; the second set was preoccupied with the other's failures, deficits, and hurtful acts. The first was involved with the inner person's deficits, and the second with the other person's deficits.

In looking at Colossians 3:9-10, Paul assumed that the Christians had actually chosen to live out of the new identity and new history, our death and resurrection with Christ:

. . . after having discarded the old worn out man [identity] with its habits, and after putting on the new one, the one being qualitatively renewed unto a personal knowledge according to the Image of its Creator (Colossians 3:9-10).

Note that Paul assumed that the old man or identity had been laid aside, and the brand new one embraced. Paul consistently emphasized that deep inner change was a slave to our instinctive self-perception. Change that perception and profound change was possible. A deep change in identity started the entire process!

Dealing with Acting Out

Dealing with painful emotions and lacks, both deep within and those stemming from relationships, was the third step in Paul's approach. The pain had to be put away. As an individual works through discomfort, lack, and disappointment with life and people in a healthy way, a remarkable thing happens. The soul is deepened and a profound sympathy enters the heart. As pain falls away, the heart can see itself and others in a clearer light. With that we come to Paul's answer to the fourth and fifth step of the addictive cycle, the initial act and acting out.

> All of you, therefore, clothe yourselves, as the chosen ones of God holy and permanently loved, with deep responses of tender mercies, kindliness, humility, mildness, long temperedness (Colossians 3:12).

If a person changes their self-perception, their identity, if they change their emotional states deep within so that they are healthier, and if they change their relationships without, so as to be at peace, it brings a person to a deep place of opportunity. It is the place of living the Christ life with others.

Paul described the kind of person who has come through the process of Colossians 3. It was a person who felt chosen by God. How does that kind of person feel? A person who has been chosen by God feels deeply secure. He or she has been chosen by the Eternal

One. That makes them safe in the arms of love that will never let go. Also such a person is holy and permanently loved. Holy means the person has been set apart by God. They will be in God the Father and Son's company forever. The other phrase is permanently loved. Many modern translations just translate it as "loved." It is more than that. It is a participle, a word that ends with *-ing,* meaning being loved, and it is a perfect participle that means that this loving will go on and on and on. The person is permanently loved.

When God loves in the Bible, it means that God enjoys the person, delights in who he or she is, has passion about the person, and that person has the caring focus of God's heart. God will forever accept and absolutely never abandon the man or woman He loves.* That individual feels like Christ when He was described at the Last Supper.

> Jesus, knowing that the Father had given all things into His hands, and that He had come forth from God and was going back to God, got up from supper, and laid aside His garments; and taking a towel, He girded Himself (John 13:2-3).

Jesus knew fully who He was at the most disastrous time in His life. He knew where He had come from and He knew where He was going. He knew Himself and He felt secure with His God. Out of that security, He could rise from the place where He was reclining and go and wash the feet of His disciples. Like Jesus the secure person is free to notice others and to serve them. He is secure enough to wash the dirty feet of others!

What Paul was describing was a process wherein the believer became secure enough to notice others, to embrace others with deep sympathy, and to serve them. This would directly answer the initial act and the acting out. The acting out is the work of the self-absorbed heart. The being clothed with compassion is the work of the other-centered heart.

---

* See my book *Becoming Who God Intended,* chapter 9, where God's love and what the Bible means by love is described.

Paul's Method of Taking Apart Addiction

This is the complete pattern we have in Paul. Note how it relates to the addictive cycle.

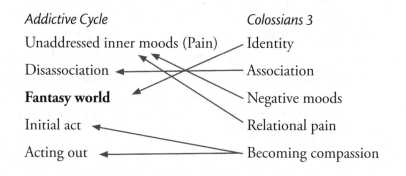

Addictive Cycle   *Colossians 3*

Unaddressed inner moods (Pain)   Identity

Disassociation   Association

Fantasy world   Negative moods

Initial act   Relational pain

Acting out   Becoming compassion

Notice again that the fantasy world is at the center of the addictive cycle, and in Paul's writing in Colossians that was the first element of the cycle that he addressed.

Kathy was working her way out of the addictive cycle. She has used food for years to deal with feelings of worthlessness and shame. Growing up she could not help but notice that her older sister was the family favorite and she often was mocked by the older sister and her parents would not intervene. She carried within some deep and powerful moods: feelings of worthlessness as an individual, and shame because she felt that she could not share with anyone her sense of rejection.

She became a Christian in college, and she was given the *Becoming What God Intended* workbook by her campus director. The material profoundly stirred her heart. She learned that she was worth a Son to God. She learned that she was delighted in by her Abba Father in heaven. She learned that out of His delighted passion for her He chose her as His daughter. Best of all she believed those truths. Over several months she noticed that her inner emotions were deeply changing. Her sense of worthlessness was dissipating, and a vibrant sense of being valued was coming into her heart. She even giggled at the thought of being special to God. As her pain level went down, she felt less and less of a need to overeat and binge.

As she saw other young women at the university struggle with food issues and family background pain, she felt a deeper and deeper sympathy for them. She decided that she could have a special ministry to those women. She decided to "clothe herself with compassion." The process of choosing a new identity in Christ, coming to terms with pain, and allowing her appetites to be managed by peace and joy, had brought her to the end result, a heart of compassion that she could wear into her relationships.

Typically the recovery movement (the movement within churches to deal with addiction) and many churches, recommend their members to join accountability groups as a means of dealing with temptation, compulsion, and addiction. Those groups are fine in and of themselves, but they have one manifest weakness. No one, including an accountability group member, can directly influence the heart. Compassion can. Compassion is the best accountability member anywhere. Always present and always powerful, compassion draws us out of ourselves. Compassion will lead men and women to think of the objects of their lust as truly human with worth and emotions, and not just playthings for the fantasy life. Compassion will help us to break through disassociation and embrace others who have the same struggles we do. Compassion was actually the most common emotion attributed to Jesus Christ in his ministry on the earth. So when we experience compassion for another we begin to experience the life of the divine. The goal of the healthy Christian life is compassion. That end goal totally overturns the addictive cycle.

We have seen that Paul's answer to the addictive cycle is a growing and thriving Christian life. The pursuit of God the Father is the most effective way of stopping the pursuit of the works of the flesh. The beauty of the Bible's approach is that it does not demand that the person "white knuckles" their way to health. Instead a growing interior focus on God through Christ creates whole new avenues in the heart.

One of the best illustrations of how addiction works is the illustration of the superhighway. When a person first is tempted, it is like he or she takes a step upon a path in the woods. One that is narrow and unused. Over time that path leads to a road. Over time that road leads to a two lane street. Over time that two way street leads to a superhighway. At the end of the process of addiction, it is like a person merging in an unbelievably quick way onto a superhighway where the traffic is going at 80 miles an hour. It is almost impossible to pull off on an exit with the volume and speed of the traffic.

The ultimate solution to the superhighway of addiction is not to build more exit ramps. Instead it is to build another superhighway in the heart. This one is a road to holiness. The first steps on the path will be strange because it will be appropriating our identity in Christ as the basis of our relationship to the Father. It will also be strange because we will have to notice the unaddressed pain in our lives. As we go from the path to the roads to the two lane street to the highway to the superhighway, it will take thousands of repetitions of the process but eventually and probably sooner than we think, we will be able to exit off of the superhighway of lust to that of holiness.

It will happen sooner than later if we embrace the new way of seeing ourselves that God has given us through Christ. The great leverage point that few seem to know about is identity. This is the great antidote to the fantasy world. In the coming pages we will see more about identity and how it is central to Christianity and true life change.

SEVEN

Unmasking Your True Identity

I was across from Al and he was sharing his concern. Al was a very bright, insightful guy, and he was anxious. Having good computer skills, he wanted a white collar job in the worst way. He was waiting on the results of an interview and he was nervous about the outcome. I asked why he was so nervous and he said it was because he saw himself as a blue collar worker who was "doomed" to spend his life working with his hands. That was his family background and that was his picture of himself.

Al further said, "I hate working with my hands. I'd love an office job." He was certainly qualified and should certainly get, if not this one another one. His emotions were controlled by the blue collar picture, and that picture was certainly false. In the same way, many lives are hindered and harmed by these instinctive false pictures. At least Al was taking a risk in the face of the false picture.

In the Cave

A passive acceptance of a false picture of ourselves is at the heart of all temptation, compulsion, and addiction. When reality and our imagination (the false picture) are on a collision course, the imagination often as not wins.

Suzanne is succumbing to temptation, compulsion, and addiction. Her life is being lived in the dark cave of sexual addiction. Some light is coming from the entrance but not enough to help. What is swirling around Suzanne inside the cave are strong desires and rampant painful emotions. Her thinking is thoroughly preoccupied with those desires and moods. At the same time on a very large screen in the cave, image after image is being replayed of past episodes with addiction. Since it is sexual addiction, the images are wildly sexual. If it were food addiction, the images would be of binging, purging, and vomiting with favorite foods being placed in the sequence. If it were gambling addiction, the images would be of card tables in Las Vegas and Reno. The gambler in the picture always wins.

Other images show up on Suzanne's screen in a random way. Scenes of childhood pain from a nasty divorce by the parents. Humiliation at work pops onto the screen. A marriage ending in divorce is there too. Those scenes just make Suzanne want the scenes of addiction to show up more quickly.

Fascinatingly with all of this going on inside, Suzanne functions often very well on the outside as an administrative assistant. Being pleasant, superficially so, and productive, in a limited way, she goes through life. For the majority of people, life is lived outside the cave, but for Suzanne as little time as possible is spent out there.

In Need of a New Family

How do we get Suzanne out? We must give her a new family life and give her a whole new set of scenes for the large screen in the cave.

Why a new family life? We have already seen through the ACE Study how significant family background is to addiction and emotional pain. In a clear majority of cases the researchers from the Centers for Disease Control and Kaiser hospitals were able to connect addictive behaviors, particularly smoking, obesity, drinking, and sexual addiction, to adverse childhood experiences. The more ACEs, or Adverse Childhood Experiences, the greater the likelihood addiction would be present in the adult life. In fact, their research concluded that addiction was a coping mechanism to deal with that pain. The goal of the addiction was to drown the pain and bring some pleasure. Suzanne has an ACE score of five. She was sexually abused, physically abused, emotionally neglected, physically neglected, and her mother was an alcoholic. Five solid ACEs was what life dealt her. Her adult health reflected the reality: She had a sexually transmitted disease, she had been date raped (the chance of a woman being raped goes up sharply with each additional ACE), and she was struggling with intermittent depression.

Introducing a New Family

Christianity offers a complete alternative to the type of upbringing that leads to addiction, and offers to deal with the effects of a high ACE score. It offers to reparent any person who decides to trust in Jesus Christ. The most powerful force on the planet to mold a person is the family, so the Bible meets the challenge of the unhealthy family head-on by bringing the person who trusts in Christ into a new family. Notice the language of John 1:12.

> As many as received Him, to them He gave the inherent right to become offspring of God, to those who are believing in His Name (His character, works, and reputation), who were born, not of blood nor of the will of the flesh, nor of the will of man, but of God (John 1:12-13).

The person who receives Jesus is the person who believes Jesus. Such a one is given the inherent right to become a child of God. Believing the gospel that Jesus died for our wrongdoing, that He rose from the dead after the third day, and believing that trust in Christ alone can make us right with God makes a person a Christian. That brings the believer into the family of God. The Greek

New Testament term for inherent right means that the individual has the essential authority to consider herself an offspring of God.

The reality of becoming a child of God is more than just the name child. Many other aspects of family life are considered to be part and parcel of the family of God. We become a close relative of Jesus Christ.

When the physical relatives of Jesus, Mary and several of His brothers, were waiting to see Him as He spoke to a crowd, He said,

> Whoever does the will of my Father in heaven is my brother and sister and mother (Matthew 12:50).

That's not a bad thing to be in a family that has Jesus Christ as the elder brother! The Bible also assumes that the great need of the person who is struggling with life can be met by getting to know and appreciate the Father of Jesus Christ, so that reparenting by this Father can take place.

Suzanne was nominally religious; she was Catholic in background, and she did believe in God. One of her coworkers told her about a pastor she knew who had been a tremendous help to her. Suzanne could see a noticeable change in Brianna, and that made her curious. She really paid attention when Brianna said that this pastor was nonjudgmental. She found that very odd from her knowledge of religious people, and that made her even more curious. Brianna shared how the pastor had helped her to understand how to deal with addictive eating, and also helped her to understand and trust God more. Finally, Suzanne could not stand it any longer and she said, "Brianna, do you think the pastor would mind if I went and talked with him once?"

> The Bible...assumes that the great need of the person who is struggling with life can be met by getting to know and appreciate the Father of Jesus Christ.

"I think he would love to talk with you, Suzanne," she said excitedly. "I will ask."

The answer came back yes, so an appointment was set up, and Suzanne showed up scared to death and yet with a small glimmer of hope.

She sat down in the pastor's office, and they exchanged pleasantries for a while. They talked about how nice Brianna was, and also about Suzanne's religious background. Then, the pastor asked what brought Suzanne to talk, and she swallowed hard and said, "I feel guilty, ashamed, and worthless. I just found out I have a sexually transmitted disease. I get involved with too many men, and I am divorced because of that." Then a huge shaking sob went through her, tears were suddenly streaming down her face, and a life story of abuse and sexual misconduct poured out. Suzanne said that she might have sex with a lot of men but she has not been able to have a good relationship with any one of them. Finally, she ended her story with a sad and plaintive, "Can you help me?"

The pastor said, "Suzanne, you have told me that you believe in Jesus and God. I'd like to tell you a true story about Jesus where He dealt with a woman who had an impossibly difficult time having a healthy relationship with men. Can I?"

"Of course," she said.

Jesus Deals with an Abused Woman

The pastor began. "Jesus was on a walking trip with His disciples and they had come close to a non-Jewish town called Samaria. His disciples went into town to buy some food, and Jesus waited next to a well for their return. As He was waiting, a woman from the town came to the well to draw water. He asked her for a drink of water. She got nervous and suspicious because she was alone with this man and He was Jewish. Her people and the Jews totally disliked each other. So she asked straightforwardly why a Jewish man was asking her for a drink."

The pastor then asked, "Suzanne, based on what you told me about your background, I suspect you're pretty suspicious too. Are you?"

Laughing she said, "Totally! What I call trust, I think is just a lower level of suspicion. I can identify with this woman."

Nodding his head, the pastor went on. "Then, Jesus said something surprising to her to get her attention, and to get her to think. He said that if the lady knew who she was talking to, if she asked Him, He would give to her living water. The woman became confused because she was listening to something that sounded confusing. She asked how Jesus was going to do that since the well was pretty deep." Then he read some verses out of John 4:

> Jesus answered and said to her, "Everyone who drinks of this water will thirst again; but whoever drinks of the water that I will give him shall never thirst; but the water that I will give him will become in him a well of water springing up to eternal life" (John 4:13-14).

"The woman did not understand at all," the pastor said, "that He was referring to something other than water. She thought He was referring to the liquid, so Jesus said that the water that He gives becomes within people a spring of refreshing water springing up to eternal life."

Suzanne was not shy, so she interrupted. "What on earth was Jesus talking about?"

"Suzanne, see if this makes any sense. Jesus did not say this kind of thing to too many people. But we will find out in the story that the woman had a really rough life, and people with rough lives often have emotional problems or are emotionally shut down. So Jesus was saying to the woman in a way that she'll eventually understand that He can give her refreshment deep within. Do you think that makes sense?"

Suzanne said, "I think so. Well the woman and I have two things in common. She's suspicious and she has emotional problems."

"In a little bit, we may see that she had something else in common with you. Suzanne, let me ask you something. You told me that one of the heartbreaks of your life was the divorce, and that was one of the reasons you wanted to talk." Suzanne nodded.

"What if I asked you to go talk to a woman who had five divorces, and she was presently living with a guy? I wanted you to help her so that she could have long-term healthy relationships with males. What would you say to her?"

"Right now all I could do was to have a good cry with her. I wouldn't have a clue!"

"Would you like to hear what Jesus said to such a woman?" the pastor asked.

"I'd love to know."

Jesus Makes an Introduction

The pastor then went on. "Jesus then asked the woman to call her husband so He could talk to him too. She answered quietly that she did not have a husband. Looking at her compassionately, Jesus said that she had answered in a very honest way because she had had five husbands and the man she was living with now was not her husband. The woman I asked you about visiting was this woman, Suzanne."

"I thought so," Suzanne said with a very slight smile.

"The woman instantly said to Jesus that He must be a prophet. But she was pretty uncomfortable with how the conversation suddenly turned to her personal life, so she tried to change the subject by asking what was the proper place to worship in Samaria where her people worshipped or in Jerusalem where the Jews worshipped."

"I change the subject too a lot when I'm uncomfortable, and I'm uncomfortable a lot. And I was waiting for you to ask me to come to your church." Then she broke out laughing and said, "In the back of my mind I was thinking, should I go to a Catholic or a Protestant church if I got serious about this God thing?"

The pastor laughed too, and said, "Let's see how Jesus answered her question. He might also be answering yours too." He then read some more:

Jesus said to her, "Woman, believe Me, an hour is coming when neither in this mountain nor in Jerusalem will you worship the

Father....But an hour is coming, and now is, when the true worshipers will worship the *Father* in spirit and truth; for such people
the *Father* seeks to be His worshipers. God is spirit, and those who
worship Him must worship in spirit and truth" (John 4:21-24).

"Suzanne, what He seemed to be saying is that it is not where
you worship but who you worship."

"That makes sense," she said, 'but I don't get what this has to do
with her man problem."

"Think about it, Suzanne. Do you think this lady came out of a
healthy home or had a caring dad?"

"Probably not. She probably had a worse dad than I had. My
dad was just indifferent to me," she said. "Something must have
really messed her up."

The pastor asked, "Would it have helped her, if she had a loving
dad?"

"Absolutely," Suzanne said emphatically, "I knew it would have
helped me."

"Well, let me tell you something really special about Jesus' response
to the woman. When He responded to her, He used the name 'Father'
three times in a row before He said 'God.' No other place in the entire
Bible does that occur. Only with this woman did He do that. Even
more exciting when He talked about those worshipping the Father
that means relying and delighting on Him, He said that the Father is
eagerly looking for those kind of people to have a relationship with.
Jesus was trying to share His Dad with the woman."

"I never thought of God as a Dad," Suzanne said.

"Many people don't," the pastor responded, "but God is a great
Dad who can reparent adults like this woman, so that they can have
the kind of emotional life Jesus promised."

"Well, I need another run at life," she said, "The first try didn't
work so well."

"Let's assume the first was a trial run, and being reparented by
the Father will be the real deal."

"I'd love that!" she said.

THE NEW REALITIES

The New Family

Jesus in John 4 gave the relationship with His Father as the beginning place for the woman at the well. Not only in the ancient world did people need healthy dads, but healthy dads are needed today. The New Testament of the Bible gives all the elements of a healthy family, a wonderful parent who is God the Father, an elder brother who is Jesus Christ, and a Holy Spirit who will make us like the family image. The Bible takes this new family very seriously and views it as the most powerful life changing experience imaginable.

Since family background is such a crucial element in temptation, compulsion, and addiction, it is very important that Christians particularly realize that living significantly within this new family is important. It is so important that Christ gave a strong admonition about realizing how critically significant this new family was.

> He who loves father or mother more than Me is not worthy of Me; and he who loves son or daughter more than Me is not worthy of Me. And he who does not take his cross and follow after Me is not worthy of Me. He who has found his life will lose it, and he who has lost his life for My sake will find it. He who receives you receives Me, and he who receives Me receives Him who sent Me (Matthew 10:37-40).

Christ has designed this statement to challenge our instincts, so that we would ask ourselves do we really think of God as our ultimate and intended Father, and God's family as the ultimate and intended family. So we have seen that Christianity is designed to give people another chance at a truly healthy family life. Billions of people on this planet need exactly that.

The New Identity

Not only do people need a new family, they desperately need a new way of looking at themselves especially if they are in addiction.

The cave's realities (see the beginning of the chapter) are so very powerful that the new family has to be combined with a whole new way of seeing ourselves.

Our family of origin creates an image for us that we often unconsciously accept. Simply put, if there is not a time in adult life where we repudiate that image, that image will be worn over our heart until the day we die. Without a time in our adult life where we repudiate that image, we cannot come to terms with life, and embrace Christianity the way we ought. If there is not a separation from the family of the origin, not the persons, but the activities and the ways of approaching life, and if new ways are not approached, dissonance and a sense of disappointment will always be present. The person will be trying to mix two families that don't fit too well.

Have you ever left home and returned at a much later time? Upon your return, you notice the constraining emotions of the past suddenly surface. After you walk into the living room, it feels like your feet are as heavy as lead and your mind slows. A very predictable set of words have to be said to your father, mother, and siblings. If somehow this instinctive pattern is not followed, one almost senses that the known universe will collapse.

Sometimes people will spend their entire adult life proving to their parents, who might even be dead, that they are not worthless. What may be driving a lot of people to perfectionism is trying to satisfy someone who may not even be on the earth any more. At some point in their life that significant parent gave them an identity, that something was wrong with them. With a desperate desire to refute that belief, they spend their adult life trying to satisfy somebody who probably did not care to begin with.

That is why we need to fully embrace the new family in Christ. It is vastly more healthy than the healthiest family on earth. The heavenly family is the one family that we will not have to get rid of baggage from. Now let us take a look at how we should look at ourselves in this new family.

The Isolation Insight

I was speaking at a Celebrate Recovery meeting at Good Shepherd Church near Portland, Oregon. The talk seemed to go well and afterward I was talking to a man and a woman who were churned up about how they were trapped in the past. The man said, "I can't seem to get beyond my emotions. I am always trapped in them when I try to deal with my past."

He was in obvious pain. An older woman was looking on and she was nodding her head. "I always seemed trapped by my past too," was her comment.

"Over the past years," I replied, "I have thought deeply about that. The person from the dysfunctional background defines himself in isolation. The person from the healthy background defines herself or himself in relationships."

When I interview people from various backgrounds and have them divided up by family background (healthy, confused, and dysfunctional), over and over again I could not help but notice what those from a healthy background would say when I asked them how they got up in the morning:

"I get up in the morning and I feel loved."

"I feel secure, and I know people like me."

"It's fun to get up in the morning."

They define themselves by their relationships. The person from the confused background will be thinking about how they might win someone's approval. But the person from the stressed background defines herself or himself in isolation. The only eyes looking at them are their own. When asked about how they get up in the morning, their replies will be like:

"I do not feel good."

"I'm depressed and don't want to be around people."

"I don't expect anything; I don't want to get up."

They don't necessarily define themselves by relationships, but they define themselves by how they feel. Oftentimes they are impervious to positive descriptions that others may use of them.

As another example of this, I was talking to Jean, and she was telling me how she was struggling with depression. She was thinking about getting off of antidepressants. As we continued to talk she said that no one liked her. I laughed and said, "Well, I like you."

"But you like everybody," she said, "so that does not matter."

"But I know a lot of people who like you in your church and among your friends. In fact, when your name is mentioned around them they lighten up. They like you.

"You know, Jean," I said, "I think that you are doing what a lot of people from a chaotic background do, you are defining yourself in isolation. Growing up you went into isolation so you would stop being hurt, and you have defined yourself by the pain of that growing up experience."

I smiled at her and said, "What I would love is to have all the people I know who like you to come and tell you why you are liked and loved. The beauty of that would be that you would not believe them. Then, if I could arrange it, I would have God the Father come in and tell you that you are worth a Son to Him. You would not believe Him either because it has not occurred to you to define yourself any other way than in isolation. Healthy people take their identity from loving relationships. Unhealthy take their identity from painful isolation."

Jean and I continued to talk about it. She admitted that was where her instincts were. We talked about how she needed to step out of those instincts and define herself by how healthy people saw her and above all by how God the Father sees her.

What we have examined creates a unique inability to understand identity, our identity in Christ. Our identity in Christ is dependent upon believing how Someone else sees us. For many that is a revolutionary thought.

The New View—A View from Above

In the view of the Bible, our self-perception should be based on how God the Father perceives us. As we accept His perception of us, a powerful new dynamic will be introduced into our lives. Before psychologists ever created the idea of self-image or identity, the New Testament already addressed the issue. In the New Testament, the image we are supposed to have of ourselves is God's view of us after we accept Jesus Christ as Savior.

Let's discover why God views us the way He does, what it means, how to emotionally derive benefit from it, what this means to us, what it means to God, and how it becomes a most powerful force in our life, particularly in the breaking of addictive habits.

Clothed with Christ

As was mentioned in the earlier chapter on destroying the addictive cycle, the heart of the challenge is the fantasy world where the imagination was used to create a false reality or identity. The answer to that was to embrace a new set of pictures of God, the world, and ourselves, a new identity. We mentioned that God gives a complete new identity to us. He wants us to see ourselves the way He sees us.

When an individual like Suzanne trusts in Christ, as she did in the first meeting with the pastor, she is clothed in Christ. Paul's letter to the Galatians, members of a church that was in what is now Turkey, used that phrase.

> You are all mature sons of God through faith in Christ Jesus. For all of you who were immersed into Christ have clothed yourselves with Christ. There is neither Jew nor Greek, there is neither slave nor free man, there is neither male nor female; for you are all one in Christ Jesus. And since you belong to Christ, then you are Abraham's descendants, heirs according to promise (Galatians 3:26-29).

When a person trusts in Jesus Christ, they are given the position of a mature adult son. They rely solely on Christ to make them right with God forever and to get them home to heaven because they have trusted that He suffered, died, and rose from the dead for them. It sounds odd to our ears that we become "mature sons of God." But to appreciate that we have to shift our thinking back 2000 years to the ancient Greco-Roman world. In that world a mature son was the person of highest rank beneath the father of the home. The mature son had greater privileges than his mother, his sisters, and the slaves in the home. A mature son had a place of privilege and freedom.

Now how did that happen? It was because God the Holy Spirit immersed us into Christ. The word immersed means to plunge us into the Person of Christ so the righteousness, acceptability, honors, and history of the Son of God are counted to be ours. That is how the Father sees us. Then, Paul the writer clarified what that means. He wrote that we are clothed with Christ. Or to put it in other words, we walk into our relationship with God the Father wearing the clothing of who Christ is and what He has done for us. He has taken away our wrongdoing, made us righteous, and given us a new family history.

New Status

Then, in Galatians Paul took the meaning of being "a mature adult son" a further step. This means that the Jew or the non-Jew (like the woman at the well or Suzanne) is treated like a mature son of God. So religious differences and cultural differences disappear when a person is clothed in Christ. Nor did being in a position of servitude, a slave, or being in a position of privilege, a free person in the ancient world, matter to God the Father. If a slave is in Christ, he is still God's free, privileged, mature son.

Nor did it matter if the person were male or female. They were still one person, a mature son in Christ Jesus. Now for many of us that sounds weird, but in the ears of the women of the ancient world that was music indeed.

Let me give an example from the modern world. In many Asian homes the most important person in the home was the son, especially the firstborn son. I do a lot of speaking in Asian-American churches. In these churches, I find the angriest women I encounter anywhere. Even though these are Christian churches, the cultural practices and instincts are still present. The angry women are usually in their 20s, and they have been treated as second-class citizens in the home. The most common complaint is that the parents went out of the way to get the sons well educated while the education of the daughters was neglected. The most interesting thing was often the young women were outraged with their moms because the mothers sided with the males and were co-conspirators with the males to deprive the daughters.

That was also the way the ancient world worked. The women were at best second-class citizens and at worst treated like slaves and property. So when Paul said that women were "mature sons" in Christ, he was fulfilling an unexpressed dream of the women of the ancient world, to have the privileges and acceptance of a mature son. That was how God was going to treat the women of the ancient world who trusted in Christ. He treated them the way He would treat His own adult Son Jesus.

Furthermore, those who trusted in Christ and who were clothed with Christ were also counted to be descendants of Abraham. Abraham was the man who was first described as being justified or made right with God by faith alone in the Bible. That was close to 4000 years ago. All of the founders of the Israelite people were his descendants and Jesus Himself is a descendant of that man. It is the most privileged family tree on the planet, and we are made part of that family tree and part of the new family of God.

All of this was gained through trust. Heaven runs on total trust; no locked doors are in heaven, nor guards, nor surveillance cameras. Since heaven runs on trust, is it any surprise that all of this is gained by trust? The one who has gained this for us is Jesus Christ. God's Son has infinitely paid for our wrongdoing by His suffering. So after God the Father raised Him from the dead, the Father just made one prerequisite for those who wanted to be all right with Him and that was to put their confidence in Jesus Christ.

A New Family History

Not only do family members look the same, but they also share a family history. God has not only clothed us in Christ but has also shared with us the central events of the Son's life on this earth. Those central events are that He suffered, died, rose from the dead, ascended into heaven, and is seated at the right hand of God the Father in heaven.

Remember when we described the video projector in the cave. Strong moods and mismanaged desires were swirling all through the cave, but the most dangerous thing operating in the cave was the video projector. That projector was projecting on a very large screen that took up a huge portion of the wall of the cave. Hurtful events from the person's past and tempting pictures to enflame the appetites were being shown on the walls. The person surrendering to temptation, compulsion, and addiction was a prisoner of those endlessly recycled video clips.

The purpose of Christianity is to burn down the warehouse of video clips and place in the projector a whole new set of clips. Those clips are of how the Father views us. Those clips become the basis of a whole new relationship to ourselves and a whole new relationship to the world outside the cave, and a whole new relationship to God.

Paul the apostle again in the book of Romans described what those new clips were and how they should influence our management of our appetites and emotions. At the beginning of chapter 6, he asked an interesting question designed to make the Christians listening to his letter think (in his time letters were intended to be read out loud). He asked them this:

> What are we saying then? Are we to continue in relationship to sin so that grace might increase? (Romans 6:1).

Paul wanted to make sure that his listeners would not misapply the principles of Christianity. For Christianity taught that Jesus Christ had made them infinitely righteous before God. Christianity taught they were worth a Son to God, that God valued them more than time, the problems that engulfed their lives, or their acts of wrongdoing, their sin. A simple application and a mistaken one would be that since we have all that grace, let us take advantage of that and sin some more! Paul wanted to make sure they did not come to that bad conclusion. So he proceeded to answer his own question.

> May it never be! How shall we who are of such a nature that we died to sin still live in a relationship to it? Or do you not know by experience that as many of us who have been immersed into Christ Jesus have been immersed into His death? (Romans 6:2-3).

Paul powerfully negated the question with a never! Then, he asked two questions that were critically important to be understood. How can a relationship to sin be sustained by those who died to sin? And the second one asked, did they not know by life experience that the person who has been clothed with Christ has also been granted the experience (from God the Father's perspective) of having died with Christ? Probably many of the first listeners to Romans were as confused by what Paul said as much as present-day Christians are confused!

The confusion comes from the difference in perspective. Our perspective is that we were never nailed to a cross, nor did we suffer on one, nor did we die there. Yet God the Father sees us that way. God did us a favor. He spared us the suffering but made us the beneficiaries of the experience Christ had. God counts us to have been on a fourth cross at Golgotha, and counts us to have died there to sin.

> God did us a favor. He spared us the suffering but made us the beneficiaries of the experience Christ had. God counts us to have been on a fourth cross at Golgotha, and counts us to have died there to sin.

Experiencing the New Family

Let me give an analogous story. A couple died in World War II in France and their one-year-old child was placed in an orphanage, but the orphanage did not know the name or any particulars about the child. So they named the child Charles, and raised the child in the orphanage. Ten years later the brother of the deceased father hunted down the child and found him. Charles had one history in the orphanage, but he discovered that he had an entirely different life history outside of it. Outside of the orphanage, he was the child of a classics professor from England and his mother was a gifted musician. He had a large extended family that had been desperately searching for him for years, and his real name was Peter Clarke. It was almost impossible for the young person to believe all of that, but over several months he started to believe and experience those truths as he proceeded to grow up in his uncle's house in England. Initially he did not feel what they were telling him at all, but over months he experienced his new family's love. After a year he was able confidently without a second thought to say, "I am Peter Clarke, the son of James and Marianne Clarke, and David Clarke is my uncle." He also inherited a new family history and a new set of relatives. As he learned this history and relied on it being true, he noticed that all of his new relatives, about 50 of them, took for granted that the history was true and Peter was part of it. He went from knowing information about his new family to experiencing his new family. He went from knowing about to really knowing his relatives.

God is doing the same for us. We have been adopted. We have a new family history relative to God, and when we rely on it and act on it we discover that it works within our new family. It works especially well with our new Dad, God the Father.

That was why Paul asked, Do you not know by experience that you have died with Christ? That was another way of saying, Have you tried out this new way of looking at yourself with God and have you experienced how well it works?

The proof is in the pudding! As we use this entirely new way of relating to God based on God's assumption that all of our sin was paid for by Christ, and we have the righteousness of God in Him, we discover that the stranglehold that sin had over our lives is broken. It is in that experience we have died to a relationship to sin.

For those who are caught up in addictive behavior, a new set of clips have to be put in the projector in the cave. The clips will be of how God sees us so that we can learn to relate to God the Father through what Christ has provided. Paul also went on in Romans 6 to tell the Christians more about their relationship to God.

> We have been buried with Him through immersion into death, so that as Christ was raised from the dead through the glory of the Father, so we too might walk in a new kind of life. For if we have become grafted or united with Him in the likeness of His death, certainly we shall also be in His resurrection, while continually experiencing this, that our old worn-out identity or man was cruci- fied with Him, in order that our body of sin might be nullified, so that we would no longer be slaves to sin (Romans 6:4-6).

Paul went on to tell the believers that not only did God view them as participants in Christ's death but they also participated in the likeness of His resurrection. It is a likeness because we did not experience it, but the Trinity counts it to be so. The purpose of this is that we should live our lives "in a new kind of life." A life where we do not live off the memories of the failures and humiliations of the past and the lusts of the present, but we live off an entirely new perspective on ourselves and a whole new set of relationships.

This new kind of life is lived by faith in a set of realities that we cannot see or feel but is based upon what is God the Father's perspective on us. This view sees us united with Christ or literally "grafted into Christ." A graft has a different origin and life than the limb it is placed into, but as it partakes of the new branch or trunk the life of the host becomes the defining reality of the grafted-in branch.

Living Out Your True Identity

Paul then applied these truths to the management of appetite and mood within. He wrote to the Romans,

> The death that He died, He died to sin once for all; but the life that He lives, He lives continually to God. Even so assume yourselves to be corpses with regard to sin, but continually alive to God in Christ Jesus (Romans 6:10-11).

The first part of Paul's thought was that Christ took care of sin once for all. The big difference between the Old Testament and the New Testament is that in the former, sacrifices had to be made all the time: daily, morning and evening, on the weekend, and many more on the Holy Days of Israel. But with the coming of the Son of God, in His death a satisfaction was made for sin that was infinite and unbounded by time.

After His resurrection, the Son went back to His Father and entered into a time of unbroken fellowship, never to be interrupted. The example of His relationship to God the Father is what is used as the standard for us. As He is alive continually to the Father so we should assume that to be true for ourselves.

It is as if God the Father and Jesus Christ are standing before us with their arms over each other's shoulders. Then, the Son beckons us forward. As we move toward them, we are not quite sure what to do. The Son then says, "Slide under our arms." You do so and you find yourself bracketed between the Father and the Son. Each of their arms is over your shoulders. The Son's right arm and the Father's left arm are resting on your shoulders. Then the Father says, "We have invited you into the circle of love that is before everything. We want you to exist within the same quality of relationship that we have with each other. In fact, we order you to accept this kind of relationship."

The command to assume that we are alive to God the Father as the Son is alive to the Father is the first command in the book of Romans. Paul has given six chapters and 11 verses of explanation.

Finally, he has reached the point where he defined for us our identity in Christ. Verse 11 now gives us the application of these truths.

A New Definition for Life and Living

Instead of assuming that our existence is defined by the swirling clouds of mood and appetite within, and the video clips of lust and pain projected on the cave walls, we are to define ourselves by how we are identified with Christ. We are ordered not to assume that we are alive to sin within, the great cave within, but instead we are ordered to assume that we are corpses with regard to it. That means we are not to focus on it, build our lives around it, and assume that it defines our existence. Instead we are to assume that we are continually alive to God in Christ.

I would argue that this is not only the first command in the book of Romans, but indeed it is the most important command in the book of Romans. In fact, I would argue that this is the most important command in the Bible for it defines our relationship to God. Our relationship to God should be the same as Jesus Christ. We have been granted the same quality of righteousness that He dwells within. That righteousness means that we are infinitely accepted and never will we be rejected.

What is so exciting is that we should no longer define ourselves relative to Him by our failure or sin, nor by the clouds of confusion and lust within, nor by the video clips of our past. Instead we can come into the presence of God as accepted the way the Son is accepted, and we can share our lives with the Father. We can come for help in time of need, and we will be received freely.

Paul particularly applied this truth to the struggle with our desires and moods within. He went on to say,

> Therefore do not let sin reign as a king in your mortal body so that you listen to its lusts, and do not go on presenting the members of your body to sin as instruments of unrighteousness; but immediately present yourselves to God as those alive from the dead, and

your members as instruments of righteousness to God (Romans 6:12-13).

It is an amazing thing that is being described here. The greatest competitor to the God of the universe, the Maker of heaven and earth, the One of all power and wisdom is our own appetites. We can either enthrone our appetites or our God. We can either deify our appetites or allow our God to be what He is, our God.

Our identity in Christ gives us complete permission to take ourselves into the presence of God. We can come warts and all. In fact, bringing our weaknesses is critical to the whole process. What we are told to do is to present ourselves immediately to God the Father, and stop continually presenting ourselves to the cave within, the cave of sin. Presenting means to come into the presence of someone and to make ourselves available to the commands of that someone. If that someone is our mismanaged appetites, if we hang around those appetites, eventually we will be following that one's orders. If we present ourselves to God the Father, and we hang around His presence the force of our appetites will dissipate. Then, a powerful prompting will come to us through the Holy Spirit, and because of the spiritual force of that prompting we will be able to obey what God wants.

This is the application of identity. Our identity in Christ, in His Person and history, gives us radical permission to live our lives accepted as He is accepted. It gives us radical permission to share our lives with the Father. It gives us radical permission to be liberated. That radical permission is contained in the phrase, "immediately present yourselves to God as those alive from the dead" (Romans 6:13).

We are alive from the dead with Christ. That being the case we do not define ourselves by what we feel within, or the history of the sins we have done without. Instead we define ourselves by our union with the Son!

Family backgrounds are a huge factor in adult addictive behavior. Transitioning from an unhealthy family background to a deep sense of one's identity in Christ and full participation in the family of God will deal with such a background. What must be remembered, though, is that no matter what the family background, the same truth applies to the person from the worst family on earth to the best family. Every Christian is ordered to live the Christian life out of our identity in Christ.

Since addiction creates a huge supply of shame- and guilt-inducing "video clips," we need to use our identity in Christ to burn down the warehouse of "clips." Instead of those old "video clips" we are to embrace an entirely new way of seeing ourselves.

The healthy Christian life is an active acceptance of how God the Father sees us. What is critical is to start using the imagination in a healthy way to see ourselves the way the Father sees us. This aggressive use of the imagination powerfully undercuts the addictive cycle.

Here is where the challenge is. We must go from information to instinct. We turn truth into instinct by believing the truth and picturing it within our hearts, and obeying the divine order that those truths should become the foundation rock of our relationship with God.

EIGHT

Dealing with Negative Moods

Doris is the university student we referred to (in chapter 1). She has become addicted to sex and the video clips that replay and replay in her mind. She was raised in a very conservative and prominent Christian family. Her parents did not know anything about the sexual abuse that male relatives in her family had done to her, and Doris did not share. But Doris sank into shame, painful emotions, humiliating memories, and hurtful pictures from the past.

Now in her later 20s she is coming to terms with the past. Interestingly only in her 20s has she learned that she is worth a Son to God the Father. She has experienced that she has an Abba Father in heaven who delights in her. And she is learning something critically important about her emotional life. If she lives under rules and laws, her inner life is devastated. If she lives under the loving gaze of her Father in heaven, she can be liberated from the emotional turmoil within. When it came to her emotional life, she had been raised with a strong moral sense. That of course made her involvement in being abused much more shameful and guilt-ridden for her, and also made it doubly difficult to extricate herself from the painful emotions within.

In these pages we will see a radical way of managing painful emotions within that Doris took advantage of, and we can too. The emotions we will first look at are the negative and hurtful emotions of shame, guilt, and worthlessness. This radical and deeply spiritual way of dealing with these emotions again is found in the book of Romans.

The seventh chapter of Romans is one of the more discussed and more mysterious chapters in the Bible. What is unique is that it is an exploration of human psychology where Paul used himself as an example. In it he shared some insights that were absolutely revolutionary in his time, and are still the same in ours. Bible teachers, pastors, and theologians debate what the chapter is about, but the major points are fairly clear. It is with the major points that we will spend our time. As one reads through the chapter, the content becomes more and more challenging. Within the first six verses of the chapter, however, Paul helped the readers out with the complexity of the material by using an illustration and three statements of principles. These principles are marvelously important for our emotional life.

The nice thing and the favor that Paul the apostle did for his readers was to start out with an illustration to help us understand the central point. We will start at the end of the sixth chapter as we step into the seventh so we have a sense of the context:

> The pay that comes from sin is death, but the gracious gift of God is eternal life in Christ Jesus our Lord.
>
> Or are you ignorant, brethren, for I am speaking to those who know the Law well, that the Law lords it over the person over the entire time he lives. For as an illustration, the married woman is permanently bound by Law to the living husband. And if the husband

died, she would be released from the husband's rule or law.
Therefore then, while the husband is living, she shall be called an
adulteress if she became involved with a different sort of man. And
if the husband should die, she is free from the Law, so that she is
not an adulteress when she became involved with a different sort
of man (Romans 6:23–7:3).

We started looking at the passage at the last verse of the previous
chapter. In that verse Paul told us that sin pays a well deserved wage
to all those who were under its sway, and that pay was death. Sin
was a system of failed effort and its destination was relational death,
spiritual death, and eventually physical death. With sin the law was
continually broken and the penalty was death. In contrast to that
was a free gift given by God in relationship to Jesus Christ and that
resulted in eternal life. Eternal life is a quality of life experienced
by Jesus Christ and passed on to us as a gift. With the first, sin, we
work and die. With the second, Christ, we are given a new quality
of life that we share with Christ. We already have endless life because
we are made in the image of God, but here we are given a quality of
life that brings us into an entirely different realm of existence. Sin
and grace then were placed in radical opposition to each other. To
further explain how different these realities were, he then gave the
following picture.

Paul gave the illustration of marriage. He addressed it to those
who have a familiarity with the Law. He asked if adultery or the
penalty for it (which was death) could be applied to a woman whose
husband had died. The obvious answer was that after the first husband was dead she was completely free. Paul by this question and
word picture wanted to make sure that his point was utterly clear.
A wife whose husband died was completely free from the binding
relationship with that husband, and she was then completely under
the new relationship of a new marriage.

He also inserted another implication. He referred to this second
man twice as a different kind of man, someone distinctly different from the first. This observation about the different husbands

connects directly with 6:23 where the payment of sin was death. In the first relationship, sin paid out death (under the legal system) when it was his reign, and in the second relationship, God the Father granted eternal life as a gift of grace. Paul's goal was to underscore through the word picture that after a dissolution of a marriage bond a new life can begin.

Principle #1: A Radically Different Relationship

Now let us examine three principles that Paul used the illustration to underscore. The first principle was that the Christian has been placed in a radically different position than what the Law offered.

> So then, my brothers and sisters, you yourselves also died to the Law through the Body of Christ, so that you will be involved with another of a very different sort, to the one being raised from the dead, with the result we would bear fruit to God (Romans 7:4).

His first application of his illustration was that the Christian has been placed in a deeply positive relationship. One not based upon keeping rules but based upon a grace and love relationship in union with one who died on the Christian's behalf.

Also Paul has a twist and a half in this principle of application. In his application we were the ones who did the dying which of course nullified the first marriage.* But we were also raised from the dead in union with Christ (a totally different sphere of existence from Paul's perspective) so that we would be joined or married to another, to Christ! A death occurred—but it was ours!

Depending on the culture a person is from, what Paul was saying here may sound very strange. The more law oriented or legalistic the background is, the stranger Paul sounds. Paul seemed to be

---

* The fact that we died was a nice way of underscoring that the Law of the Old Testament has not disappeared. It has a place and application, but it just does not apply to a Christian as a rule of life. The Holy Spirit is our Ruler of Life.

implying that the Law was not a very good thing to be under, and that we needed deliverance from it. What did he have in mind?

I was teaching a singles' retreat near Mount Hood in Oregon. The singles were an older group so I asked them how many of them had been married. Nearly every hand in the group went up. Then, I asked how many of them had been married to not very nice husbands. Since the group was mainly women, a good number of hands went up. Then, I asked who among them (it was a fairly large group) had been married to a second husband who was much nicer.

An older woman who looked very Italian raised her hand. I asked her to describe her first marriage. "My first husband was very critical," she said, "and he had nothing good to say about me. He was always pointing out my faults and humiliating me."

"Were you happy in that relationship?" I asked to draw her out more.

"I was miserably unhappy," she said. "He eventually died of cancer and I took care of him through the entire time. Even on his deathbed he was criticizing me."

"Tell me about your second husband."

"He passed away too, but he was wonderful. He was always kind to me, and we were married for ten years," she replied with a smile. Then, she said with this wonderfully happy expression on her face that made her lovely beyond her looks, "He thought I was beautiful."

"With your second husband," I asked, "would you do anything for him?"

"I would because he was wonderful. I loved to do things for him," she said.

God's purpose in joining us to Christ was to place us in a relationship that would draw the best out of us. Like this woman's experience, any person who is under any legal, religious system (it does not have to be a poor form of Christianity) can't help but be discouraged and unmotivated. Sooner or later the person will end up deeply criticized because all the rules can't be kept all the time.

The Father wanted to draw the best out of us so He placed us in a gracious, kind relationship with Someone who was not a score-keeper. He took us out of the world of rules and grafted us into His Son. The purpose of that was that we should have fruitful lives.

We must not base our relationship with God on moral rules. We have been placed in a totally different relationship to sin and the Law, and it is absolutely necessary to understand what that different world is. In a sense, the difference is like this. A farmer in the 1920s was given a Ford Model-T car as a gift. He did not know how to drive and he did not want to learn, but his grown children gave him this gift and he did not want to seem ungrateful. So he hitched his two farm horses to the car, and had them pull the car everywhere he wanted to go. Well, in the same way, many Christians are hitching the Law to the Holy Spirit and the new realities we are in and are trying to live that way. So Paul used the illustration of the married woman to underscore his principle that we are not under the Law but we have been joined to Christ.

Principle #2: Rules Don't Work!

Paul then gave the negative reason or principle as to why we should avoid placing ourselves under the Law. This reason has endless implications for dealing with temptation, compulsion, and addiction. If there ever was a truth we needed to get our arms around, it is this one.

> When we were continually in the flesh, the powerful negative moods which belonged to the sins, which moods were produced through the Law, were working continually in our members with the result of bearing fruit to death (Romans 7:5).

Every Christian should clearly understand what Paul was saying here. Understood, this principle will force believers to reorient themselves completely in the Christian life. Paul was speaking of how he and others functioned under the Law prior to their conversion. Paul used the phrase "in the flesh" to refer to the time prior to Christ.* During that time overwhelming, powerful emotions produced fruit for death. Paul said that these powerful overwhelming emotions also belonged to sins.

In a fascinating way, Paul assumed that behind every sin (note that the word sin is in the plural form in the verse) was a maelstrom of powerful pushy emotions. These emotions were obviously not the fruit of the Spirit, love, joy, and peace. Instead they were a complex mix of pain and desire. What created the inner catastrophe was the surprise. The rules of the Law did!

The particular rules of the Law did because the Law expressed itself in concrete rules. It was not the Law in general but the rules in particular that ignited this emotional force.

> They had not realized that their guilt was pouring gasoline on the fire of desire...The rules were unleashing an unstoppable force that would drive them toward acts of sin.

Earlier today as I was writing this chapter I had an extreme example of this shared with me. I called a church in California and asked for one of the pastors but I did not identify myself. The lady who was fielding the calls recognized my voice, and asked if this was David Eckman. She said that she was regularly listening to our audio material and so she recognized my voice. She had worked there for years and I knew her somewhat, so we started to talk. She said her own personal ministry was leading a small group with women who were struggling with same-sex attraction.

She said the tapes were very helpful to her and the women. She learned from the tapes that the force of the sexual desire was driven by the shame and guilt over the same-sex attraction. Prior to listening to our lectures and the audio material, the women said

---

* Paul said we who are Christians should not walk "*according to* the flesh" (Romans 8:4), but he went on to say very clearly that Christians were not *in* the flesh (Romans 8:8-9). We can choose to live our lives in harmony with the flesh, but we are no longer encased and surrounded by the flesh.

that they were just being driven to become more sexually preoccupied with the same gender. Prior to listening they had not realized that their guilt was pouring gasoline on the fire of desire. They had not realized what Paul was saying that the rules were unleashing an unstoppable force that would drive them toward acts of sin. The rules against lesbianism created such pain that they were grabbing instinctively for the pain killer of lesbianism.

The Law Problem

The rule actually made the failure and immorality far worse. In fact, it drove the individuals in the direction of the sins themselves. The law agitated the flesh to produce powerful emotions and sensations within. Take the law out of the equation and the pressure would be reduced precipitously. The steam would be drained out of sin's boiler. Later in Romans chapter 7, Paul used his own life to illustrate this principle.

> What shall we say, then? Is the Law sin? Certainly not! Indeed I would not have known what sin was except through the Law. For I would not have known what coveting or lusting really was if the Law had not said, "Do not lust or covet." But sin, seizing the opportunity afforded by the commandment, produced in me every kind of covetous desire. For apart from law, sin is a corpse. I was once alive apart from the Law; but when the commandment came, sin became alive again and I died (Romans 7:7-9).

Do you remember the old black-and-white movie *The Invisible Man*? When I watched it, I was seven or eight years old. The coolest part of the movie was when the invisible man wrapped himself in bandages before going outside. The bandages made him visible as he put on a hat, sunglasses, and an overcoat and went out. Without that outfit the man was invisible.

Without the Law sin is invisible. One of the great purposes of the Law is simply to show us that sin exists and what it is. Paul the apostle insisted that was a critically important ministry. But the downside is that Law (and not the next exciting principle that Paul introduced) has an enflaming effect on my emotions and desires, and a crippling effect on my character. The reason is because I am relating to a rule and not having a relationship with God.

The Law stirs the embers of the waning fire of sin within. For regarding sin and Law, Paul said, "For apart from law, sin is a corpse." The opposite world to the Law is grace. Under grace properly applied, sin loses its power and ceases to be a living force in the believer's life.

Therefore, it is critically important to get people who are struggling with temptation, compulsion, and addiction not to orient themselves to God based on Law. The guilt, shame, and worthlessness produced by the Law will drive the tempted person in the direction of their desires to get a "quick fix" and not in the direction of God the Father. Dramatically Paul wrote with force, "The sting of death is sin, and the power of sin is the law" (1 Corinthians 15:56). The inherent strength of sin comes from a rule. It enflames the desires and drives the person with guilt and shame.

Principle #3: Life in the Spirit

The alternative to the preoccupying force of the rules of the Law is the reign of the Holy Spirit. Paul in verse 7 drew the previous two principles together and joined the third to it.

> Now we have been released from the Law, having died to that by which we were bound, so that we serve in a new quality of Spirit and not in the worn out oldness of the letter (Romans 7:6).

The verse said again what Paul has repeated frequently and affirmed in his illustration of the woman and her husband: The Christian is not under the legal system of the Law.* Then, he also stated that we have died to that system by being identified with the death and resurrection of Christ. Quite a dramatic thought that the

---

* Paul said that we are not under Law or the rules of the legal system frequently (Romans 3:20,21; 3:28; 4:13,14-16; 5:20; 6:14-15; 8:2-3; 10:4; Galatians 2:16,19,21; 3:11,13,17,21,24; 5:4,18; Ephesians 2:15; Philippians 3:9; 1 Timothy 1:9). Instead we are under the sway of the Holy Spirit so that we might produce in cooperation with Him the character we need.

first husband did not die, but we died instead and were raised from the dead so that we could be joined to another. And the nature of our resurrection with Christ is so significant that we are placed in a different realm entirely that Law cannot reach.

This realm is not where we have to check an old worn-out law code that is 3500 years old, but instead we are to live a life where the new quality of life comes from the Holy Spirit Himself. The Trinity has provided for us richly. We have been given a "Dad" in heaven, a Redeemer on the cross, and an indwelling Person in the Holy Spirit. What is more powerful—an archaic piece of writing or God? Yet multitudes of Christians reach too, too often for the faded piece of manuscript and do not turn to the Father God so as to be empowered by the Holy Spirit.

Many in the throes of temptation, compulsion, and addiction are desperately looking for a solution not only in all the wrong places, but out of pure religious sincerity they are looking for the solution in the worst possible place—the Law. Such sincerity becomes their worst enemy. They think that if they keep the rules (even though they have failed magnificently at doing so), they will find release. It is like a jungle explorer who goes on a date with an anaconda. He embraces the anaconda affectionately! The harder he embraces the snake, the tighter the coils of the anaconda get. The explorer is embracing his own demise. Again that is what Paul said, the strength of sin is the Law (1 Corinthians 15:56).

The Choice We Face

We have a similar choice as Adam and Eve did. In Genesis 3 they had a choice between a fruit on a tree that was good to eat, pleasant to the eyes, and able to make one wise—or a relationship with God. The choice was between something good and God. They chose good over God. Their choice was not seemingly for something evil over God, but something good that God had made. Their choice led to death because embracing the good meant abandoning God.

The Christian has another choice between a good thing, in this case the Law, and God. We can embrace the Law or we can embrace God. To embrace the Law means that we do not believe that the living God is capable of producing character and happiness apart from rules. It is ludicrous to believe that rules are better than God, but practically speaking multitudes of Christians have believed that, and acted on it. In one sense, it is like saying to one's wife that an evening with a good romance novel is much better than an evening with her. The conclusion of those comments may be death!

So Doris, the woman mentioned at the start of the chapter, liberated herself from sexual addiction by not trying to be moral, but instead by taking her immorality to the Father in a transparent way. She learned that she was delighted in by the Father; she discovered in an emotionally rich way that she was worth a Son to the Father; she discovered by sharing the video clips in her mind with the Father they lost their effect, and then she discovered she could start dumping them in the dumpster, so to speak, and leave them there.

She stopped making the mistake of desperately trying to be moral. Instead she realized that morality was a by-product of a healthy relationship with God the Father. We have the silly thought that if we are moral then God will help us to be more moral. The reality is that we are just never moral enough. At every point we must come to the Father with the empty hands of faith. But those hands have to become empty after we have dropped our failures in the presence of God.

A STRATEGY THAT WORKS IN EVERYDAY LIFE

Let us put the three principles of Romans 7:1-7 together in one spot. They are as follows:

1. *A radically different relationship.* By our union with Christ, we have a radically different relationship to God

the Father. Rather than a rules-based legal relationship, we have been placed in a totally grace-based relationship.

2. *Rules don't work.* A preoccupation with rules leads to explosions of addiction. Add to that guilt and shame, and the Christian or non-Christian becomes completely powerless—and sin becomes overwhelmingly strong.

3. *Life in the Spirit.* God's alternative is to bring our failures into His presence so that we can get help in time of need. The help we get is the Spirit's power. The process involved is the spiritual life pattern of Colossians 3. Out of our identity in Christ, we relate to the Father. We put to death our moods and appetites. We remove relational pain and put on compassion.

Our emotional life can become crippled by a preoccupation with the Law. But life produces many other emotional hurricanes. Those storms can be just as crippling as shame and guilt. Those storms also will drive millions to take shelter in the arms of addictions. Let us see how the truth of the Bible brings those stormy winds to calm.

Pain from Family Background

As we have seen from the Adverse Childhood Experiences Study, painful experiences from the past directly affect the health of adults. These experiences not only affect health, they also directly affect the emotional life. Much of adult depression can be traced to what people have experienced in their growing up years.

In the fourth chapter of this book we discussed how family backgrounds influenced adult health. We looked at adult depression and how a direct link exists between depression and family background. The research of the Centers for Disease Control and Kaiser Permanente concluded that. We showed charts from the study that showed much of addictive behavior had such connections.

Then, the Kaiser hospitals decided that they would see if they could be helpful to people who participated in the study. They brought in those who were suffering from chronic depression in adult life for a one time talk with a therapist. The role of the therapist was simply to ask the person about their family background and whether that person thought a connection existed with the depression. The therapist did not do formal therapy. All that was done was to seed the thought that a connection might exist and find out what the patient thought.

The result was that for the following year, doctor's visits went down 50 percent! I heard that statistic, and I thought maybe the patients simply did not want to come back because they did not want to talk about their family background. So we wrote Dr. Felitti, the Kaiser internist who was in charge of the project, to see if that might be the case. Responding, he said that a number of his fellow physicians thought the same thing, so they decided to ask the hundreds of people who were interviewed what they thought of the interview. It was done by mail and they gave them a form to mail back.

Dr. Felitti said that 80 percent responded (which was an unheard-of high percentage). Overwhelmingly the respondents were delighted with the interview and they said it was greatly helpful. The stark proof of their happiness was the drop of 50 percent of medical appointments. Dr. Felitti went on to write to us that helping people to come to terms with their family backgrounds would constitute a major medical advance.

What the Centers for Disease Control and Kaiser hospitals found is just a few flecks of ice on the tip of the iceberg! Every adult carries within herself or himself painful baggage from the family of origin causing pain and ineffective painful relationships.

I believe the church has an immense opportunity to do very consciously and intentionally what it many times does almost by accident. Almost accidentally the church tells its members about their identity in Christ, the relationship they have with an Abba Father in heaven, and the powerful Person of the Holy Spirit. The more astute or needy church members may grab onto those truths and undergo a deep transformation. According to my research about 95 percent do not. That high percentage has an inner life still controlled by the family background instincts. At best those instincts were buried under mounds of good biblical information. Those instincts will pop back up through the mounds and control the life when the pressure and stress is great enough.

The church not only can help Christians and non-Christians come to terms with their family backgrounds, but it can help the millions who suffer from long-term depression and as a result, they become compulsive and addicted.

The Pain of Depression

Let me help you see how to approach this challenge. I was talking to a number of people who suffer from long-term depression. Most are women. What was interesting about them was they completely assumed the emotion of sadness and negative thoughts was their identity. That's who they are. Somehow the depression and negative thoughts were superglued to their person.

Now as a proviso I sincerely believe and our organization maintains that at a certain point when struggling with depression, it is wise to take antidepressants. I tell those individuals to take the pills to the greater glory of God, and thank God that we are so fearfully and wonderfully made that we can be helped through many different avenues. In this case, the avenue is chemical. Combine chemicals with biblical truth delivered by a trained counselor and for many that is a blessed combination.

The depressed person needs to realize that they are doing what many people from a dysfunctional family background do. They are defining themselves or generating their identity in isolation and aloneness, a crucial and understandable mistake. The healthy person defines himself or herself relationally through the loving eyes of near and dear people. Unhealthy depressed persons frequently define themselves in the critical eyes of those who have mistreated them and who left them confused about themselves. Then, the depressed person takes a further step and makes the resulting emotional pain their essential identity. "I am my pain," they believe.

Bill and Sue have been dropping in on the Setting the Heart Free Seminar that I have been teaching at Peninsula Bible Church for several weeks. They have been financially supporting our nonprofit ministry for many years. The reason is that about ten years ago Sue stepped out of the "quicksand" and looked Jesus in the eyes and saw herself reflected there. What she saw was a loved, whole, valuable person. If He sees her that way, she could see herself that way too.

A profound change came into her emotional life and her husband Bill became a "fan." He saw and experienced the change. Sue of course had a deeply unhealthy background and for that reason she refuses to have a picture of her father in her home. He had deserted her, and she then defined herself as worthless (reasonable enough thing for a child to do). Then, she further defined her identity by the pain of depression wrapping its tentacles around her soul. Everything changed when she looked at herself through the eyes of God the Father and Jesus.

Pamela, a missionary wife, was in the audience in a Southeast Asian city where we were putting on the same Setting the Heart Free Seminar. She came up and said 12 years ago she attended this same seminar in California.

"My husband and I attended Dallas Seminary," Pam said, "and we helped start a church with one of the finest and best known Bible teachers in the United States. None of that helped the guilt, fear, and depression that I was experiencing. Then, I attended this seminar, and I believed what I heard and the changes have stuck." Her words illustrated the reality that depressive instincts will always trump the best information.

"Could you share what you just said to the people who are starting this seminar as a way of encouraging them to really pay attention?" I asked.

She did and she emphasized to them how important it was to see ourselves the way God the Father sees us. She experienced how spiritual truth integrated into the mind and imagination was ignited by the Holy Spirit for long-term change. Chronic depression often is the chronic feeding on the pain from a false picture of ourselves. Her presence and words were a real gift from God to me because we were just starting a series of seminars in this important Asian city.*

In some ways the pain of dysfunctional family backgrounds and the pain inflicted by the Law is similar. In both the Law and the unhealthy family background, people are being told of their short-comings. In both the Law and the unhealthy family, people are being driven into shame. In both systems, people end up feeling worthless. In neither system are affectionate eyes reflecting back to them a positive picture.

In some ways the greatest gift a healthy set of parents can give to their children is an honest and affectionate picture. But for most people that has not happened. At best for many the picture is confusing. The church can step into that lack and tell everyone how God the Father sees them. The church can lead if it wants in the "reparenting" process.

In previous chapters we have described what is needed to be believed and embraced to initiate change. The first step of course is to embrace and believe the love of God. That love was recommended to us on the cross. When we were at our worst, God the Father decided to give the greatest gift, His Son (Romans 5:8). Essentially the cross says that God has such a delighted passion for us that He will set aside our sin (while taking it seriously by giving a Son for sin) in order to establish a relationship. He values us more than He abhorred our sin. Such love for our person is the basis of the divine romance. If we buy that, a deep sense of appreciation should develop.

---

* This series is also part of an e-learning course called Spiritual Life Development, which is described in the back of the book.

We have looked at the pain from placing ourselves under the moral expectations of the Law as opposed to a living relationship with God the Father. Furthermore, we have seen also that family backgrounds can do the same to us. The Law is a system and the family background creates a system within the inner life. Both can be devastating.

Now we want to look at other sources of pain. What's left is the flotsam and jetsam of emotions. But that debris can be very powerful, and it can push people in the direction of addiction.

Paul in Colossians 3 described emotions that were of two types: negative moods or emotions that corrupted the heart and negative moods or emotions that corrupted relationships. Both types of emotions can generate enough pain to drive addiction. For example, relational pain and the deep grief that results in bitterness, wrath, outrage, and ill feelings "can drive a person to drink." Or negative moods, such as anxiety, loneliness, and boredom, to name a few, can set up the initial step of the addictive cycle. Sometimes relational pain is more obvious because it revolves around persons, but whether obvious or not pain cannot be left unaddressed. So the two types of unaddressed pain are 1) pain of the inner life, and 2) pain of the relational life.

Pain of the Inner Life

Paul spoke to these two areas in Colossians 3. We will first look at the pain of the emotional life, and then at relational pain. Paul named three types of painful corrupting emotions: those of eroticism, those of strong painful moods, and those of various forms of covetousness.

> You immediately put to death, therefore, your members which are upon the earth, with regards to sexual immorality, sexual uncleanness, negative mood, wrong desire, and greed which is idolatry (Colossians 3:5).

Eroticism is painful because sexual desire intrudes into places it does not belong. A brutal example would be a father's sexual misuse of a daughter. The lust is satisfied and the interior of the girl's soul has the battery acid of guilt, shame, and worthlessness poured upon it.

A strong painful mood is like anxiety. The anxious person is always living under threat. Where a healthy person sees a solvable problem, the anxious person sees imminent disaster. That is a terrible way to live. Another painful emotion Paul mentioned was greed. The greedy person lives in a world of lack. They do not have a Father in heaven who actually notes their needs and sends the encouragement and care of heaven. The greedy person has the mind of the Depression-era orphan who had no dad, government, or relatives to watch out for the person. But the greedy person wants, and is in painful desire because contentment never became a friend. Greed then is obviously intermixed with anxiety.

Dealing with Anxiety

Jesus considered anxiety as something that deeply and negatively affected the human life:

> Watch yourselves, so that your hearts will not be weighted down with hangovers and drunkenness and the anxieties of life, and that day will not come on you suddenly like a trap (Luke 21:34).

Notice how addictive behaviors are connected with anxiety. The combination weighs down the heart so much that it loses its spiritual alertness and the judgments of God come suddenly and destructively without being anticipated. Jesus presented anxiety as a significant threat. Anxiety is a negative mood that affects the heart dreadfully. It is not a desire for anything but it is an emotionally painful rut that the heart falls into.

People who have become habituated to anxiety only notice it when it is overwhelming and often debilitating. But the way to deal with anxiety is to become well acquainted with its first appearance and put it to death as Paul said in Colossians 3:5. God is concerned about our hearts, and He does not want us to wallow in such pain. Anxiety as such is a significant issue in Scripture. An anxious person lives in a world of threat, and the way out is for the anxious person to transfer themselves to a different kind of world, a world under the care of God.

> All of you quickly humble yourselves under the mighty hand of God, that He may exalt you at the right time, after having cast all your anxiety on Him, because all of you are a concern to Him (1 Peter 5:6-7).

The anxious person must transfer themselves to God's care, and not stay in the world of threat. The Bible points to the great care and power of God as something for the believer to rest in. His care will work itself out considerately and will bring great positive good into the life.

The command to be humble is to allow God to work in our lives for good. Humility is a belief that we need the help of Someone else to be effective in life. Nothing will stop God's good intentions from working out more than our own willingness to drown ourselves in our anxieties. On a perfectly sunny pleasant day, the anxious person is throwing herself into a boiling uncomfortable cauldron.

To stop throwing ourselves into the cauldron, a process exists that we need to know well. Otherwise we will find ourselves in the pain of anxiety and driven in the direction of temptation, compulsion, and addiction.

When we realize that anxiety is not our destiny, the process begins. It is not something we are to live under and in. Paul emphasized stopping anxiety. In order to do so we would have to recognize anxiety being present and the need to deal with it. If we don't, we open ourselves to addiction.

> Do not allow yourself to continue in anxiety, but in relationship (to all anxiety) by prayer and petition after thanksgiving, let your specific requests be made known to God (Philippians 4:6).

First, the Christian needs to begin communicating concerning the anxiety but in a way that asks for help. Then, a specific request for help needs to be shared with God concerning the threat behind the anxiety. The more specific, the better.

This, however, has to be accompanied by thanksgiving. For true thanksgiving to occur the heart of the anxious has to decide who is bigger: the enveloping problem or the all-powerful God. If the anxious person entrusts himself to the threat, the anxiety will skyrocket. If God is trusted, then true thanksgiving can begin. So the request for help has to be preceded by the exercise of faith. The heart has to say to God the Father, "I will entrust this threat to you. I will ask for this specific help to deal with the threat." Ultimately life does not depend upon us, but life depends upon a surrender to the goodness of God.

> The man or woman who is using sex or food to deal with the anxieties of life now has a better option....A caring Abba Father is in heaven, and the problems of life can be shared with Him.

The result of sharing these anxieties with the Father in a believing way is the peace of God. Such surpasses all comprehension and will guard the heart and the thinking process (Philippians 4:7). The word for guard was often used of a Roman garrison protecting a city. An immediate peace would start seeping into the heart and a protective peace would start protecting the heart. The person should pray until he or she is peaceful. It is not the technique that matters but the results. When peace arrives, the heart is out of pain and addiction is thwarted.

The man or woman who is using sex or food to deal with the anxieties of life now has a better option. Anxieties and threats can now be met through relationship. A caring Abba Father is in heaven, and the problems of life can be shared with Him. Numerous women including June have shared with me how having a reliable source of peace and tranquility has taken the need for "grazing" or nervous snacking from their lives. What they have done is apply the peace of God to the first step of the addictive cycle. But to do that they had to deal with the threats in the world around them through a vital relationship with God the Father. But it all starts with recognizing that anxiety is no friend.

Pain of the Relational Life

Relationships often bring pain. When a relationship goes sour, the deeper the friendship the deeper the pain. Well-intentioned people hurt others as well as certifiably evil people. Relational hurt then is another source of pain that often is unaddressed and wears like acid on the soul.

One look at the Adverse Childhood Experiences Study (the ACE Study) immediately surfaces the prevalence of relational pain. The so-called ACE factors have an obvious relational component to them. ACE factors such as physical abuse, emotional abuse, physical neglect, emotional neglect, and the observed physical abuse of the mother in the home, all speak of hurtful relationships and pain. All this pain sets up the child to find relief in addictive behavior. Then, family background pain spills over to adult life and contaminates adult relationships with bitterness and mismanaged emotions. Then, the adult either comes to terms with that pain or heads in the direction of addictive behaviors.

So the pain the tempted, compulsive, addicted person may be dealing with may have started ten minutes ago with an explosive argument with a spouse or it may be the decades-old experiences of growing up. Whatever the start time for the pain, the challenge is still the same. The pain needs to be dissipated and tranquility restored.

Anger

Paul made an issue out of relational pain by dealing with its symptoms: anger, rage, malicious talk, bitterness, and lying in Colossians 3:

> Even now all of you immediately take off (like clothing) all of
> the following: anger, angry outrage, malicious feelings, slander,

shameful speech from your mouth. Stop lying to each other after having discarded the old worn out man (identity) with its habits, and after putting on the new one, the one being qualitatively renewed unto a personal knowledge according to the image of its Creator (Colossians 3:8-10).

He called the Christians he wrote to, to address the relational chaos that existed in their lives. As always Paul said this putting off has to be in harmony with the new identity that they have in Christ. The new identity brings with it a sense of security and love that reduces a person's need to bludgeon their way to happy relationships. Sadly the angry person has the illusion that people are won by inflicting hurt on them. It does not work.

Instead of the steam of anger the individual needs the security, tranquility, and compassion that comes in Christ. Out of those qualities they will have a far better chance of enduring enjoyable relationships. How does Paul say we should deal with the residual pain of rotting relationships? He gave the answer further on in Colossians 3.

All of you, therefore, clothe yourselves, as the chosen ones of God, holy and permanently loved, with deep responses of tender mercies, kindliness, humility, mildness, long temperedness (Colossians 3:12).

Deep responses of tender mercies, simply known as forgiveness, truly applied out of a heart that is feeling loved and secure reduces relational pain. Without forgiveness, there can be no resolution. Otherwise the people we refuse to forgive will almost have a demonic force in our lives. We will be preoccupied with them and tormented by them maybe even years after they have died.

Forgiveness

True forgiveness means that I have to revisit the damage that I was caused. See it for what it is, and grant forgiveness or the withholding of punishment upon those who inflicted the damage. For the Christian the best way of doing this is to use the imagination. The Christian should picture himself or herself in front of the cross with Christ dying upon it. Off to the left is the damager and the damage the person has caused.

In front of the dying Son of God, the Christian chooses to accept the damage the damager has caused because Christ has died for the Christian and the victimizer. That process and picture may have to be repeated dozens of times before it becomes real. But as it becomes an emotional reality within the person's life, liberation from pain occurs and peace comes into the soul. We forgive others first because it befits what Christ has done for us. Second, it benefits us because it gets the poison of bitterness out of our hearts. Third, the person we forgive gives us the privilege of doing to them what Christ has done for us. Fourth, the person who hurt us is forgiven. In the context of this book, the most important thing about forgiveness is that it takes away the pain that may start the addictive cycle.

Dealing with pain is critical in dealing with addiction. We have seen that pain has many sources. The most surprising source is that the Law itself generates mountainous waves of pain within those who build their lives on Law. That pain unleashes the incredibly fierce power of sin within our lives. To deal with that we have to live within the grace that is in Jesus Christ.

Other sources of pain exist. Pain comes with the family backgrounds of many and also the present relationships of life. Reduce the pain and addiction may well cease. Pain also comes from how we manage our inner life. If we do not deal with the anxious cares afflicting us, we may again find ourselves in the pursuit of pleasure to drown the discomfort.

Pain is not the inheritance of the child of God, blessing is. We discover that blessing as we turn to the God of all comfort and the Father of every mercy to meet the needs within and to abate the pain within. To deal with pain ultimately means that we become very well acquainted with our Father God.

The goal of being human, and the goal of being a Christian is not just to be a person who does right things, such as not succumbing to addiction. Ultimately life is not about handling the chaos within. A deeper purpose exists for our hearts to enjoy and a deeper purpose inhabits the universe. The deeper purpose for everything is to enter the circle of love that has predated time. The circle of love is the relationships existing within the Trinity, the love shared by the Father, Son, and Holy Spirit. We have been made in the image of God and as such ultimate realization of who we are is found in the heart of God.

The goal of being human is to have a romance with God, and such a romance is the best addiction proofing defense possible. We cannot always live our lives on the defensive afraid of what we will become, and what we will do wrong. When the positive and noble is pursued, life is lived best. In the coming chapters we will see that the ultimate defense against temptation, compulsion, and addiction is a growing Christian life.

THREE

ADDICTION-PROOFING THROUGH DEVELOPING A ROMANCE WITH GOD

NINE

Getting God's Word into Our Heart of Hearts

The ultimate advantage of addiction-proofing is not the death blow delivered to addictive behavior, but the great release of the power of a positive spiritual life. A healthy spiritual life should be the result of addiction-proofing. When addiction-proofing is completed, the heart is filled with the pleasures of God, and the pleasure of God.

As we have discussed in the previous chapters, addiction creates a superhighway in the mind that the addict is driven along or pushed along at high speed. Once on it, it is difficult to get off. But as the addict gets off every once in a while, the best defense against that old superhighway is to create another superhighway in the mind—a great romance with God!

A very standard way to build a superhighway in the mind in the evangelical church is regular Bible reading. This is a wonderful and great thing to do. Many of those most used by God the Father have been those who have a great familiarity with the Bible. To be steeped in its truths, is the way to live heaven's life in the here and now. A love of God and the love of the Bible go hand in hand.

Information Versus Integration

Yet the Bible is frequently misunderstood and misused. And it is in that misuse a vulnerability is created that can be taken advantage of by sin and addiction. Let me share a simple illustration. In the previous chapter, we referenced 1 Peter 5:6-7.

> All of you quickly humble yourselves under the mighty hand of God, that He may exalt you at the right time, after having cast all your anxiety on Him, because to Him it is a concern for all of you.

I can memorize the two verses, and someone can check on me to see if I have it correct. If I do, I will have achieved a simple goal, memorization, but I have not achieved the goal of the verses.

The goal of the verses is to remind me that those emotional feelings of anxiety are the property of God (He wants to take possession of our fears and release us from them), and I should return God's property to Him. To do that, then, I need to sense the fear within. I also need to recognize that much of life is out of my hands, so that I have to surrender to the overwhelming, prevailing power of God. Doing that, I will certainly run into resistance from my own heart and will. Almost certainly my heart would love to solve its own challenges and not rely on anyone else including God.

To memorize the verses takes short minutes, to integrate the verses into my heart and emotions may take months. The second, integration, is vastly more important than the first. To integrate is to defeat addiction. To merely memorize is to create more of the fantasy world where we think knowing information is a substitute for living out the information.

Much of the Christian culture reads the Bible as information, while the Bible's authors have a much different way in mind. The Christian culture's way actually presets people for the addictive cycle by making them emotionally vulnerable. We can see the vulnerability in the example from 1 Peter. If I *learn* a verse, I may naively think I am *living* the verse. That is dangerous. The danger lies in the fact that instincts will always trump information. If I assume memorizing it has changed my heart, I may be greatly mistaken.

The addictive cycle works completely out of the instincts. When the addicted person feels pain, he or she will instinctively disassociate, and enter the fantasy world. To deal with that the Christian has to learn to instinctively take the heart's pain to God the Father for comfort and resolution. So the question is: Are we using the Bible to train our mind or to train our instincts? How we answer that question will determine if we can deal with addiction.

Well, then, how should we understand and read the Bible? We will answer that question not only on how it applies to dealing with addiction, but also how it applies to the normal Christian life. Part of the purpose of this book is to maintain that the normal vibrant Christian life is the best addiction-proofing there is.

IDENTITY: THE BIBLE'S MOST CRUCIAL FRAMEWORK

Often the Christian culture's way of reading the Bible is built around fragmenting verses out of context, ignoring the emotional realities the Bible addresses, and missing the intentions of Scripture. When the Bible is read contextually with an eye out for its emotional implications, and in submission to its purposes, then the Bible becomes a powerful weapon against the addictive cycle.

A crucial example of the contextual use of the Bible regards the truth of our identity in Christ. In Ephesians Paul wrote of the need to put on the new identity in Christ. As that was being done, the old man or identity had to be put off.

For many Christians the knowledge of their identity in Christ is not well known. Or if it is known at all, it is just another scrap of biblical information thrown into the hopper of their minds. We all have driven by tree trimmers who are feeding branches of trees into their shredding machines. They feed the branches into the machines. There's a great sound of shredding wood and leaves, and the chips are blown into the back of a truck. Well, the truths of the Bible, for many believers, land like those wood chips in the back of their minds and lie there in a big pile (which eventually starts to decay). No organization, no hierarchy, no interrelationships exist. Just scraps inhabit the mind. As a result, the centrality of the truth does not grip them, nor is the significance of it for their lives realized.

The Bible works differently. Coherence, interrelationship, and order adorn its pages. We can see this, for example, when the letter to the Ephesians is examined carefully, identity is central. Let us take a look at where the verses about our identity in Christ fit into the context of the whole book.

The Old Versus the New

In Ephesians 4:17 Paul wrote that the Ephesian Christians should not be living their lives the way the Gentiles, the non-Christians, do in an aimless way with a darkened understanding. Instead, they were to do as they were taught which was to put off the old identity.

All of you, put off according to the former habits the old worn-out man [identity], the one continually deteriorating according to the lusts of deception, and allow yourself to be made new in the spirit of your mind, and put on the qualitatively new man [the new identity], the one having been created in harmony with God in righteousness and the sanctifying process of the truth (Ephesians 4:22-24).

Three realities were being addressed at the same time. The first was that the Christians had an old way of living and perceiving themselves that needed to be set aside. That perception was directly connected to habits and sensations. Paul called those things "the former habits" and "the lusts of deception." Obviously the old man or identity was strongly tied to the habits of life and the habits of appetite. As that old perception was set aside the assumption would be that the habits of life would be directly affected and the habits of appetite would be also. Lusts and old habits appear to be like Velcro stuck to this instinctive picture of ourselves. Change the identity and the old habits and deceitful lusts will go with it.

This putting off would be in partnership with the Holy Spirit who wants to renew the Christian's mind so as to make it brand new. The goal would be that the believer was no longer living off of the fumes of the past. Furthermore, in cooperation with that renewal the Christian was to put on the new identity. This new man or identity was qualitatively different than the old worn-out man. The term for new Paul used referred to a qualitatively different identity. So the Christian's mind was to have a brand-new start and the Christian's new identity was to be qualitatively different than the one in the past.

What we have here is very similar to what we looked at in Colossians 3 where Paul placed living out of the new identity as the starting point for dealing with the moods and appetites within (the addictive cycle). But what we want to do with this portion in Ephesians is to show how central and critical it was to Paul that Christians understand and live out of the identity in Christ.

A Coordinated Wardrobe

What we will do is to take a look at how these verses, 4:22-24, fit into the context of Ephesians. Why is this important? It is important because, as we have said repeatedly, many Christians live their lives dressed in tattered scraps of Bible verses and Christian truths. They are not dressed in the new identity in Christ. They are dressed in scraps of unsorted information.

In contrast to those scraps, the Bible isolates some truths as vastly more important than others. For example, the truth about the Trinity is infinitely more important than the account of the genealogy of Christ in Matthew. In a very real sense, the knowledge of our identity in Christ is at the top of the pile of truth. It is not as important as the existence of God, but it does explain the nature of our friendship with the God who exists.

Let us see how this portion of Scripture fits into the context of Ephesians. Ephesians is a letter that is divided up into two parts. The first dealt with how much the Father loves us. The second dealt with how we can respond in a worthwhile way.

Ephesians

1-3: God's wonderful treatment of His own

    1. His love for those He chose

    2. His union of Jew and Gentile in Christ

    3. Paul's role in this revelation

4-6: Our worthwhile response

It is not unusual for Paul to evenly divide up one of his letters in such a way. He did a similar thing in the letters to the Colossians and Romans. In the middle of his letters, he often will make a major transition to a related topic. Starting in Ephesians 1, he described how from eternity God the Father has involved us in His love. The Trinity has brought us into their circle of love, and we have been embraced by the love of the Father, the protection of the Son, and the assuring presence of the Spirit.

This relationship was extended to both the Jew and the non-Jew (Gentile) and a new kind of humanity was created, the body of Christ. Chapter 2 described the great benefit of that truth: We have equal access to God. In chapter 3 Paul went on to describe his own mission of bringing the truth of the Body of Christ, and its place under the grace of God into the light. Then, Paul went on to pray for his readers that they would make their lives a comfortable home for Jesus Christ, and they would experience the great depth of Christ's love for them.

Those first three chapters contain a list of incredible blessings that the Christian has:

1. We have grace and peace (1:1).

2. We have every spiritual blessing in heaven (1:2).

3. He personally chose us in love before time (1:4).

4. We are destined to be full-grown daughters and sons of God (1:5).

5. We are graced in the Father's beloved One (1:6).

6. We have the redemption of the Kinsman redeemer through Christ's blood (1:7).

7. We have been forgiven for those times we have refused to do right (1:7).

8. We have been given a portion in God's great purposes (1:11).

9. We were protectively sealed by God's Holy Spirit (1:13).

10. We were given the Holy Spirit as a nonreturnable down payment (1:14).

11. We have been given spiritually enlightened eyes (1:18).

12. We have the incredible greatness of His power directed for our good (1:19).

13. We have God's great mercy extended to us due to His great *agape* love (2:4).

14. We have been made alive together with Christ! (2:5).

15. We have been permanently saved by God's grace (2:5).

16. We have been raised up and seated with Christ in the upper heavens (2:6).

17. We will be objects of His grace into eternity (2:7).

18. We are permanently saved as a gift not our own efforts (2:8-9).

19. We are near to God by the blood of Christ (2:13).

20. We have peace with God in the Person of Christ (2:14, 17).

21. We have had the commands of the Law nullified (2:15-16).

22. We have immediate access to the Father through the Spirit (2:18).

23. We are fellow citizens with the saints and members of God's household (2:19).

24. We are being built into a home of God by the Spirit (2:22).

25. We who are non-Jews are fellow-heirs, fellow body-members, and fellow-partners in the Christ (the Messiah) (3:6).*

26. We have the unlimited wealth of the Christ (3:8).

27. We have friendship, access, and confidence through faith in Christ (3:12).

28. We may have the overwhelming power of God in our inner life (3:16).

29. We may become a home for Christ through faith (3:17).

30. We may have an unlimited experience of the *agape* love of Christ (3:18-19).

31. We have the experience of God doing more than we can ever imagine (3:20).

A careful review of the above brings to light an incredible treasury of grace and blessing in Christ. From Paul's perspective the lives of Christians are flooded with the grace of God. Our wealth

---

* The Messiah (the Hebrew word means "the anointed one") of the Old Testament, and the Christ (the Greek word means "the anointed one") of the New Testament come together in the Person of Jesus. All the Old Testament and New Testament promises regarding the anointed one are ours in Him.

is not the resources that we have in the bank. Our resources are the privileges we have been granted with the Father, Son, and the Holy Spirit. Paul described those blessings in detail in the first three chapters of Ephesians.

The Way Christ-Clothed People Act

Then, he transitioned to how we should respond to them. Ephesians 4:1, the middle of the letter, made the transition.

> I am continually encouraging all of you, I the prisoner of the Lord, to immediately order your life in a manner worthy of the calling by which you have been called (4:1).

What followed his exhortation was a series of applications to how this grace we have received should be applied to life. An outline of the last three chapters is as follows:

Transition: 4:1 "Let us walk worthy!"

Chapter 4: Responding in a worthwhile way

    4:1-6 Sustain the seven Trinitarian unities

    4:7-16 Participate in the growth process

    4:17-21 Our first personal responsibility—put on the new identity

    4:22-33 Be people of truth

Chapter 5: Become imitators of God, walk in love!

    5:1-14 A call to ethical growth

    5:15-21 Walk wisely as Spirit-filled people

    5:22-32 Walk wisely as married people

Chapter 6: Walk and stand!

    6:1-4 Healthy relationships with children

    6:5-9 Conduct of slaves and masters

    6:10-24 Stand in the cosmic struggle against evil

Paul applied the grace of God the Father to the following sequence of ethical responsibilities. At the end of chapter 4, he told the Christians in Ephesus to be people of truth. Then, he said in chapter 5, the Christians should grow ethically, particularly as Spirit-filled people, people who were having their deep needs and areas of pain met by the Holy Spirit. Then, the wives and husbands were challenged to live a married life worthy of Christ (5:22-32).

Then, in chapter 6, he applied the call to a worthwhile walk to the relationship of children to parents (particularly commanding fathers to be nurturers) and parents to children in the home. From there he transitioned to the relationship of slaves and masters. He ended chapter 6 with a trumpet call to the church in Ephesus to stand in unity like a Roman cohort against the assault of the devil and his malicious spirits.*

A Key Point Where Our Response Is Needed

Those ethical sections are preceded by 4:1-21. The elements of those 21 verses prepared the way for the applications that followed.

Chapter 4: Responding in a worthwhile way

     4:1-6 Sustain the seven Trinitarian unities

     4:7-16 Participation in the growth process

     4:17-21 Our first personal responsibility: put on the new identity

Paul described three realities: the Trinitarian realities that established the church, the process of growth sustained by the church,

---

* Ephesians 6:10-20 described a Roman cohort of 280 legionnaires coming under attack. Often North American caucasians and blacks read it as a description of a gladiator, one man under attack. But every "you" in the passage is plural so it is comparing a church to a cohort. Furthermore, the description of the armor in Greek was of the weapons of a Roman soldier. Finally the defensive tactics of standing against attack was quite characteristic of Roman battle tactics.

and the first ethical responsibility of believers. That first responsibility preceded all the other responsibilities that followed.

Paul, first, described the realities creating the church, the body of Christ. Those unities were the one body of Christ, one Spirit creating its life, one hopeful calling, one Lord of the Church, one content of the faith, one immersion in Christ, and one God and Father of all. These seven realities created the warp and woof of the church. Those elements of love created a new people on the earth, the body of Christ. Those elements gave the "ethnic identity" of the new people. Each member of the Trinity was related to the new people: God as a Father, the Son as the Master or Lord, and the Spirit as the life-giving presence.

From the seven realities, Paul went on to the growth process of the church. The growth process was built around the gift of apostles, prophets, evangelists, and pastors and teachers (4:7-16). The goal of these gifted individuals was to bring the people of God to a maturity that brings glory to God. As Christians respond to the ministry of these leaders in a healthy way, the Body of Christ will grow quantitatively and qualitatively.

So far Paul has given the dimensions of this new body, the body of Christ, and the process of growth within that body, the ministry of gifted leaders. From there he transitioned to tell believers what they needed to do to participate in a healthy way. What he called the believers to was written in 4:17-24. The heart of that has to do with the embracing of the new identity.

> All of you, put off according to the former habits the old worn-out man [identity], the one continually deteriorating according to the lusts of deception, and allow yourself to be made new in the spirit of your mind, and put on the qualitatively new man [the new identity], the one having been created in harmony with God in righteousness and the sanctifying process of the truth (Ephesians 4:22-24).

What all of us need to notice and integrate is that embracing our new identity has to precede the practice of Christian principles.

Before we address our need to be Spirit-filled so as to deal with the pain and weaknesses of life, we need to begin to live out of our identity in Christ. Before we address the complex challenges of family and social life, we must fully embrace how God the Father sees us in Christ. When we face the onslaught of the devil who wants to convince us that we are unloved, abandoned orphans, we must clothe ourselves in Christ.

How Paul and Jesus Blast Apart the Fantasy World

Notice how the central challenge of the fantasy world in the addictive cycle is directly addressed by the central truth of the Christian life, our identity in Christ. A normal Christian life is God's answer to the addictive cycle. Many Christians are defenseless against addiction because they do not have a clue as to what is central in the Christian walk. Many Christians who end up in addiction have taken their basic identity from the addiction and not from the Bible. That is a tragedy.

> For many Christians and church leaders a truth like our identity in Christ is a luxury item...Such a truth is not optional—it is a spiritual and psychological necessity.

For many Christians and church leaders a truth like our identity in Christ is a luxury item. Not everyone has it, they seem to think, but for those who do, it is a nice thing. Instead, such a truth is not optional—it is a spiritual and psychological necessity. Everyone has an identity. It would be good if all of us had the identity that God wants for us.

Since the center of the addictive cycle is living out of a fantasy world that justifies addiction and even makes it a necessity, it is quite fascinating that the Bible would pursue the same reality. Spirituality, then, as we have been saying, is a frontal attack on the addictive cycle.

We have seen so far that Colossians 3 (chapter 6), 1 Corinthians 6 (chapter 2), and this portion in Ephesians 4 base the Christian life on our identity in Christ. Over and over again in the writings of Paul, identity is the strategic center of Paul's understanding of the Christian life. If we take a close look at Paul's writing, the place of identity is given central place. The following is a list of places in Paul's writings where identity is crucial. Usually they are central chapters in the book. Many of them have been discussed in this book or in the companion book *Becoming Who God Intended.*

- Romans 6: This chapter is the critical center of Paul's development of the Christian life.

- 1 Corinthians 6: This chapter gives the way out of addiction, our unity with Christ.

- 2 Corinthians 5: The chapter speaks of how everything is changed because of our union with Christ.

- Galatians 3:26–4:31: Again our unity with Christ is the basis of all.

- Ephesians 4: Putting on our identity with Christ precedes the practice of the Christian life.

- Philippians 3: In this chapter Paul gave the motives that drove his life, and not surprisingly it revolves around his union with the Son.

- Colossians 3: Our union with Christ puts to death the moods and desires of the flesh.

The remaining letters of Paul are either shorter or they are dealing with specific issues of the life of the churches and ministry within them. What we have seen with Paul is also reflected in the pivotal gospel of the four gospels, that is the one by John. The fourth gospel often is called the spiritual gospel because it is not as concerned with the events of the life of Jesus as it is with the meaning of Christ's life.

The richest section of teaching in John is chapters 14 through 17. That section is after Jesus washed His disciples' feet and left the Upper Room. It is the evening before His crucifixion, and He shared in its most direct form the heart of Trinitarian Christianity. He gave the roles of the Father, the Spirit, and His own place within the new relationship He was establishing.

Then, in chapter 15, He gave the parable or picture of the Vine and the branches. Jesus is the life-giving Vine and the believers are the branches. The responsibility of believers is to draw upon the life of the Vine to sustain them in this new life.

> I myself am the True Vine,* and my Father is the farmer or vine-dresser (15:1).

> I Myself am the Vine, you are the Branches. The one continually remaining in a relationship to Me, and I in him, this one will be bearing much fruit, because apart from Me you are not able to be doing anything (15:5).

Nothing can happen that is meaningful in the Christian life or in the churches apart from our union with Christ. Living out of that unity does not happen by accident, but it is done by a conscious decision to put off the old way of looking at ourselves and embracing God's new way of seeing us.

Living out of our identity in Christ is the vital center of everything in Christianity. It is not a teaching for the few; it is the teaching for all. Where is this teaching to be applied? It is to be applied to how we function inside ourselves. We have seen how crucial identity is. Now we will take a quick look at how concerned God is about our inner life, so that we see God wants the Bible integrated into our lives and not just memorized.

---

* Jesus Christ was the True Vine, and this is most certainly in contrast to Judea, the false vine of Isaiah 5, which bore, to God's disappointment, sour grapes or fruit.

THE BIBLE REVEALS CONCERN
FOR OUR DEEPEST HEART

Our heart is God the Father's concern. For He knows that from the heart flows the issues of life (Proverbs 4:23). We have seen that the issue of identity is a critical one. We will now take one of many examples to show that the inner life is also consistently addressed by the Bible. The God of the Bible is not just concerned about what we do (indeed that is important) but also about what we are on the inside, and the relationships we sustain.

Earlier we have looked at the story in the gospel of John concerning the woman at the well. We have seen how Jesus addressed the desert of her emotional life, and showed her how she can have a spring within leaping up to the experience of eternal life. We will take another example from the ministry of Christ, and then make observations about God's preoccupation with what happens within us.

Jesus Is Not Impressed

The story from the gospels that we will look at is the story of the rich young ruler. The story appears in three of the gospels (Matthew 19:16-30; Luke 18:18-30; Mark 10:17-22). Matthew tells us that the man was young; Luke tells us that he was a ruler; Mark tells us that he was rich. We will look at Mark's account mainly because it has a unique and revealing feature.

> After He proceeded on the way, one came running to him and after kneeling, he was continually asking Him, "Beneficial Teacher, what shall I do in order that I should inherit eternal life?" (Mark 10:17).

The rich young ruler displayed a commendable humility. He bowed before Jesus and made his request. He also called Jesus a "beneficial teacher." That would appear to be a compliment. But Jesus did not appear to be overly impressed.

Then, Jesus said to him, "Why are you calling me good or beneficial? No one is good except God" (Mark 10:18).

In my imagination I can almost see the disciples blanching or
turning white. Jesus has just challenged, if not insulted, a very rich
potential donor and also someone who if angered could become a
political threat. I can picture them saying to each other, "Well, He
went and did it again!"

Jesus essentially questioned the young man's request and pushed
it back in his face. The young ruler used a term that meant beneficial, and he also asked what he could do or perform so as to
have eternal life. The implication was that Jesus was being viewed
as a reward dispenser for good behavior. The young man was not
treating Him as God, but as a vending machine. In my mind's eyes,
I see Jesus asking with irritation why the young man was calling
Him beneficial. Obviously Jesus implied that the man did not know
what he was talking about.

Also Jesus seemed to be distancing Himself from God. The
normal way of taking the statement that no one was good except
God was to assume Jesus was saying that He was neither good nor
God. But that remains to be seen as the story goes forward.

Jesus also gave him a follow-up set of comments concerning
the Ten Commandments. "The commandments you know," Jesus
said. "Do not commit adultery. Do not murder. Do not steal. Do
not give a false witness. Do not defraud.* Honor your father and
mother."

The man responded that he had guarded every one of those
from his youth. Matthew 19:20 tells us that this was a young man
probably in his 20s. So the period the ruler referred to was relatively
short. But this second time when the man responded, he called Him
just a teacher and left the word "beneficial" out. He was not going
to repeat his previous mistake. But it was also obvious to him that
Jesus was not impressed.

---

* This one was not part of the Ten Commandments, but it may have had a particular relevancy to the
rich young man. The term *defraud* was frequently used of withholding the wages of poor workers.

A Merciful Challenge

What is important to notice was that Jesus quoted from the second half of the Ten Commandments. That is often called the second tablet of the Law. The first half dealt with what belongs to God and with what God expected with regards to Himself. The second half dealt with how human beings should be treated. The rich young ruler said that he did a great job in his treatment of his fellow human beings. Then, the gospel of Mark has a most interesting comment about Jesus that was not in the other two gospels.

> After looking at him carefully, Jesus loved him with *agape* love, and said to him, "One thing you are lacking. Go, whatever you have sell and give to the poor people, and you shall have treasure in heaven, and come follow me" (Mark 10:21).

Jesus had a deep personal reaction to the man. It is unusual in the New Testament for a personal comment like this to be made about Jesus that He loved a particular individual. The disciples, however, noticed something in Jesus' interactions that reflected an emotional connection and caring on Jesus' part. A shift had occurred in Jesus' interactions with the man. Earlier Jesus had challenged the man and almost certainly made him feel uncomfortable about using the title "beneficial." Now Jesus was going to make him more uncomfortable, and as He did so an obvious tenderness had entered into Jesus' voice and demeanor that the disciples easily spotted.

On the surface the young man appeared to be a very moral person. He also appeared to be a humble and religious person because he had approached Jesus with humility, and asked for something that seemed to be spiritual. But Jesus obviously wanted no part of it. He compassionately addressed a great demand to the young man. After hearing it, the man became shocked and deeply depressed. Then, he went away never to be heard from again as far as the pages of the New Testament are concerned.

A number of important observations come out of this story. The first dealt with the divinity of Jesus. Jesus initially challenged the young man's superficial assumptions about good and God. Then, He asked him about his performance of the second tablet of the Law (the commandments dealing with people). Blithely brimming with confidence that he had kept all of those rules, the man certainly assumed that he would gain the approval of Jesus. Instead Jesus made a God-like demand of him. Jesus asked the young man to sell everything he possessed, and come and follow Him.

He gave the ruler a choice between his idolatry and the divine Son. What the challenge of Jesus exposed was the idolatry of the man. After the individual stated he was thoroughly moral, Jesus drove him to become better acquainted with his heart. Having a choice between God as represented in the Person of Jesus and his own wealth, he chose his wealth. Unknown to himself until Jesus confronted him, his heart had endlessly broken the first commandment of not having any gods next to Yahweh,* the God of the Old Testament.

> You shall have no other gods in front of Me. You shall never make for yourself an idol, or any likeness of what is in heaven above or on the earth beneath or in the water under the earth. You shall never adore them or serve them; for I, Yahweh your God, am a jealous God, visiting the iniquity of the fathers on the children, on the third and the fourth generations of those who are hating Me (Exodus 20:3-5).

Jesus' claim to divinity was implicit in the entire story. At the beginning of it, with the searching questions about the word good or beneficial, Jesus forced the man to really think about what he had said about Jesus. Then, He faced the man with a choice between his idolatrous love of his wealth, and His own Person. The man sadly chose his idol.

---

* *Yahweh* is the personal name of God in the Old Testament. Sometimes we see the name spelled *Jehovah* and pronounced as such, but Yahweh is a more accurate rendering.

A Crisis of the Heart

The ruler was plunged into sorrow and depression. In front of him were eternal life and a teacher who obviously had profoundly impressed him. Inside of him was the shock of discovering that he was addicted to his wealth. He was called to surrender that wealth, and it was emotionally impossible for him. The depth of his slavery drove him into shock and depression. Discovering his addiction and how it limited his heart from following Jesus, he was stunned.

Jesus had created a massive crisis for him. Coming to Jesus, he expected a revelation on how to have eternal life. Leaving Jesus, he had a revelation of the life of his own heart. The words used to describe him are shocked and depressed. Having seen his heart, he was shocked.

Sometimes the best thing that God can do for us is to introduce us to ourselves and then to allow us to sink into pain. On the one hand, the text stated that Jesus had *agape* love for the man. Jesus delighted in who he was; He valued him as a person; He wanted his highest good. On the other hand, He plunged him into pain. Sometimes the best thing God can do for us is to push our hearts into shock and pain. Pain, therefore, may be as we said in earlier chapters a great gift of God. Furthermore, God's love for us always goes deeper than the pain we may be in. Jesus looked through the young man's pain and saw someone He loved.

Up to the time the young man met Jesus, he did not realize how desperately he was clinging to his wealth. He started with a crisis of religiosity and Christ put him into a crisis of the heart.

The important thrust of this story was Christ's concern for the man's inner life. The young man viewed Jesus as a dispenser of goods and one of those goods was eternal life. Those assumptions in one sense were quite correct except one critical element was missing: The man did not know what was going on inside of himself. He did not know what he really needed which was to be delivered from idolatry. Without that knowledge, any request that he made of Christ would be missing the point.

The young man in this story and the woman at the well were walked through the same process. In both cases Jesus introduced both of them to their own insides. With the woman he emphasized that she needed a whole new emotional life. She had to acquire something. With the young man, he needed to let something go from his inner life, his idolatry. In both cases, they were crippled by what was going on in their emotions and desires. In both cases, Jesus knew what was there and the two appeared to be clueless. He had to introduce them to themselves.

Disclosing the Inner Life

In the same way, when a person is involved with temptation, compulsion, and addiction, he or she may not realize what is actually going on inside of the heart. More often than not, the addicted person is hardly aware of how quickly after they sense the initial discomfort or pain they jump into the addictive cycle. The church's ministry and the pastor's and preacher's ministry should be the same as Jesus which is to introduce people to what actually is going on inside of them. This story of the rich young ruler, like many of the biblical stories, is preoccupied with what people have going on inside of themselves. God is interested in our addictions because He wants to rescue us from the pain and appetites within. We were created to know Him, and not to serve them.

The story of the rich young ruler can be multiplied over and over again in the pages of the Bible. Nathaniel, Nicodemus, the synagogue rules, the seven churches of Revelation, and many other people and portions underscore the truth that God is interested in our inner life. We can now take a look at where in the Old and New Testament this was said directly.

The Bible Gets to the Guts of the Matter

We have seen so far that God is terrifically interested in what is going on inside of us. The entire context of Ephesians and many other portions underscored that very powerfully. We not only need to know how to manage our insides so as to deal with the addictive cycle, but we need to be able to do that so as to meet the basic expectations of Christianity. Also such stories as that of the rich young ruler are saying the same thing, our hearts matter to God. Now we will look at that principle repeated over and over again that God the Father is interested in what is going on in us.

God the Father has a great interest in us integrating truth into our hearts as opposed to just placing information in our heads. A friend of mine coined the word "graphomania." *Grapho* means a written word, and *mania* obviously means insane. The word was coined to describe the person who has an insane interest in the words of the Bible and not necessarily any interest in integrating those words into the heart. The God of the Bible is determined to make sure that our *hearts* reflect His Word. One of the Proverbs reflects that reality:

> The refining pot for the silver and the furnace for the gold, but the One testing hearts is Yahweh (Proverbs 17:3).

The refining pot and the furnace place great heat on the metals. Their purpose is to greatly improve what is there. What went into those pots comes out better after the process. In the same way, the God of the Bible takes the human heart and puts it through a process of stress. When He is done what entered is better after it leaves the process. The word for testing contains the truth that God is doing this all the time.

The Darkest Recesses

Jeremiah the prophet was very aware of this reality and a number of times in his book he described God as the one who searches and tests the inner life. In fact, it was expressed in a unique way.

> I, Yahweh, continually search the heart, I continually test the kidneys, even to give to each man according to his ways, according to his deeds (Jeremiah 17:10).

God is a God of reality. He wants integration. What we do should be in harmony with who we are. So He continually deals with what is going on within us. In the Old Testament, physical organs of the body represented what was going on in a person's inner life. The heart represented the center of who we are and where the great decisions of life are made. That was the place of relationship and will. The kidneys were further down and in the back. They represented in Hebrew thought the deep recesses of a human being. That was their equivalent to our unconscious, the deep and dark recesses of the soul. Yahweh, then, was the One who was continually searching our relationships, our will, and our consciousness, but He was also testing the deep aspects of our being that we are hardly aware of. Does what goes on within us matter to God? Of course!

> God is a God of deliverance, and He very much wants His children to experience this deliverance.

This same thought is connected with Jesus Christ in the New Testament. In the book of Revelation, Jesus, the ascended Lord of the churches, is examining the life of various churches.

> I will kill her children with pestilence, and all the churches will know that I am He who continually searches the kidneys and hearts; and I will give to each one of you according to your deeds (Revelation 2:23).

The same thought appears in Revelation that is in Jeremiah. God wants to see what is in the depths of who we are. He is not satisfied with mindless, robotic obedience. He then will reward those who are deeply faithful to Him within themselves, hearts and kidneys, and faithful to Him in their outward activity, according to their deeds. What is a marvel about biblical ethics is that it makes a spectrum of demands upon us. It wants consistency through and through.

God Wants the Real Person

What was true in the New Testament was also true in the Old. For example, in the wilderness wandering of the people of Israel when they came out of Egypt was a time when God wanted to discover what was in their hearts. This not only applied to the individual but to the entire nation. The God of the Old and New Testaments always wants to know if He was dealing with the real person within or just a bundle of lusts, desires, and uncomfortable emotions.

> That being so, you shall remember all the way which Yahweh your God has led you in the wilderness these forty years, that He might humble you, testing you, to know what was in your heart, whether you would guard His commandments or not (Deuteronomy 8:2).

The reality of what was in His people was so important to Yahweh that He would allow specific tests to come into the lives of the people. For example, he would permit a false prophet or a false dreamer of dreams to bring wrong revelation to His people to see if they were really deeply in love with Him.

> You shall never listen to the words of that prophet or that one dreaming those dreams; for Yahweh your God is testing you to find out if you are continually passionately delighting in Yahweh your God with all your heart and with all your soul (Deuteronomy 13:3).

In one sense, He put His people at the risk of failure so that they would know and He would know the reality of their inner life.

※

The point of this book is that a vibrant Christian spirituality is the answer to the addictive cycle. The tragedy is that most of evangelicalism is very far from the heart of Christianity. How can we say that? A minority of Christians know about their identity in Christ. A small minority of those Christians have integrated that truth into their lives. In addition, the recovery movement (the movement to deal with addictions) is viewed as an add-on to the life of the church. The recovery movement should be the church. The recovery movement assumes that people have deep struggles within which leave them powerless. That is one of the basic tenets of Christianity: we really are weak sinners. The recovery movement also assumes that the truth of Christian spirituality has to be deeply applied to those needs.

What is the challenge that has to be overcome? It is the challenge of "graphomania," or believing that *knowing* the biblical information is more important than *applying* the biblical information. Often we are people of great illusions (the fantasy world is alive and well). The great evangelical illusion is that believing the truth is the same as practicing the truth. Truth known is not necessarily truth integrated.

We have seen three realities that challenge "graphomania":

1. The New Testament demands spirituality that deeply addresses the inner life.

2. The entire Bible shows that God has a preoccupation with spiritual reality in the inner life.

3. New Testament spirituality presumes a Christian lives out the relationship with God through their identity in Christ. To do that the heart has to be profoundly changed.

So the Bible has to be used as a means and not an end.* Our hearts are deceptive enough to convince us that all we need is the information. That, if believed, will produce sorry tragedies. God is a God of deliverance, and He very much wants His children to experience this deliverance. He is so intent upon that goal that He has given His Son for our rescue and the Spirit for our empowerment.

---

* I have contributed a chapter to the book *Who's Afraid of the Holy Spirit?* edited by M. James Sawyer and Daniel Wallace. This whole issue of the misuse of the Bible and the non-use of the Holy Spirit is addressed in detail.

TEN

Communication That's Sensational

Addiction is the theme park of the lonely. The park itself is the fantasy world, and the addictions are the rides. But unlike other parks such as Disneyland or Great America, the theme park of addiction has only one person in it, the addict. If the afflicted person has grown up in a dysfunctional home, she or he wears loneliness like a second skin. So being alone in the park seems very normal to the rider on the roller coaster of addiction. When in pain, the individual does not turn to another. Instead she turns within and enters the theme park of the mind. But between the emotional pain and the entrance to the park exists disassociation. To be in the park the person needs to choose non-relationship.

The role of the Bible is to attack disassociation and to foster the relationship with God the Father. Not existing as an end in itself, the Bible exists to bring us into the kind of relationship that Jesus has with the Father. Much of what is in the Bible is to convince us that we can have a relationship with God. Before we dare speak and relate to God, it helps to know that we have access and welcome. We have to assume His arms are open before we run into them.

Reckoning on a Relationship

Rarely do my wife, Carol, and I have an argument. As we have gotten older, strife has been less and less. If emotional disagreements can be kept few, a happy marriage for 35 years can happen. Early in our marriage we did have a few arguments and often with them came "freeze outs." A freeze out is when after heated words, I would decide to ignore Carol. I would not focus my attention on her. We might have been in the same room, but we were not assuming the other person was. In fact, if we were in the kitchen, I am sure I paid more attention to the food in the refrigerator than I did to her. I was assuming that she did not exist.

It sounds silly, but before I can relate to someone I need to assume that the person exists and I have access to him or her. I have to reckon on the individual's existence. Then, if I believe I am able to associate with the person, I may. It is like riding the Bay Area Rapid Transit in San Francisco. I may have a thousand people around me, but I can pretty much assume very few are wide open to a conversation. But if I see a friend on the train, a good conversation will certainly happen.

So in the same way with people, it is with God. Before we have a talk, we need to assume He is there and He will relate to us. The Bible actually orders the Christian to make that assumption that God is there and is ready to relate. We have seen earlier in Romans 6 that we are commanded to assume we are alive to God the Father. When we make that assumption or we reckon that to be true, we address the issue of disassociation.

> The death that He died [referring to Christ], He died for sin once for all. And the life He lives, He lives to God. Thus [as He is alive to God] also you yourselves assume or reckon yourselves to be corpses on the one hand to sin, and on the other hand continually living to God in Christ Jesus (Romans 6:10-11).

We are ordered to assume that we are as alive to God as Jesus

Christ Himself is alive to the Father. We are not to assume that we are alive to sin within, but instead we are to assume we are just dead bodies with reference to sin.

A relationship with God works so much better when we believe that such an important Person wants to be our friend. Actually He would like us to assume we are family members. That is what God wants us to reckon. We are to assume ongoing access to the Father. Access is an important word in the New Testament and the Greek Old Testament. In the Greek Old Testament,* access referred to the right to see the king at any time or to come into the presence of God in the tabernacle and temple of the Old Testament. Paul stated we have such access in Romans 5:2 and Ephesians 2:18 and 3:12. Peter used the verb that comes from access to describe what Christ has done for us.

> Because also Christ once for all suffered concerning sins, the righteous one on behalf of unrighteous ones, with the result that He could bring us into the presence of God (1 Peter 3:18).

Paul ordered us to assume such access and Peter told us what Christ did to obtain such access, He suffered once for all. Previously we have said that Romans 6:11 was the first command in the Book of Romans and we have argued that it may well be the most important command in the Bible. Everything else flows from the assumption that we have a living relationship with God and it always exists.

When someone is in a home by herself, she will not look for anyone to talk to in the empty home. If the phone rang and she expected a friend to be calling, she would lift the receiver up with expectancy since she was looking forward to the chat. God indeed is also available to chat. Christ has moved Him into our lives and homes.

Different Bible books say the same thing different ways. For

---

* The Greek Old Testament, often called the *Septuagint,* was a translation of the Hebrew Bible into Greek made between 300 and 100 BC. Much of the vocabulary and usage of the New Testament also appeared in this translation.

example, the book of Hebrews emphasized that this open and transparent access is through the blood of Christ.

> Having then, brothers, confidence (like speaking to a good friend)
> for the entrance or access to the Holy Place by the blood of Jesus
> (Hebrews 10:19).

Our character did not gain access for us. The work of Christ did. Because of that blood of Christ, we have the open invitation to come to God the Father as we are through what Jesus has done for us. We can speak to the Father as to a friend with transparency and confidence that we are welcome and He will help us.

Communication Based on Heart Conditions

We are to use our access to develop a healthy prayer life. In Christian bookstores a multitude of different patterns for prayer are available. But in some ways the Bible has reduced the practice of prayer down to its simplest elements. In studying the Old Testament the rabbis concluded that no set pattern for prayer existed in the Bible. As a result, unfortunately they went out and invented one! The requirement was that prayer should be made three times a day no matter where you were. So some rabbis strategically placed themselves on crowded street corners at noon. The purpose was to be seen by those about them. Jesus ordered his disciples not to be like them, but instead to privately pray to their Father in heaven (Matthew 6:5-6).

What some rabbis failed to notice is that in the great book of prayer in the Old Testament, the book of Psalms, prayer to God was largely a result of oppression and desperate need. The most common type of psalm was a "Lament of the Individual." Coming out of great anguish, the psalm was a desperate cry for help. The concerns of His people were what God wanted to hear. The God of the Old Testament obviously is the same as the New for in both parts of the Bible what Peter said was true, "It is a concern to Him about all of you" (1 Peter 5:7).

When should we turn to God in communication and request? Obviously when we are in pain and need. James says it simply and well.

> If anyone is suffering wretchedly, let the person pray, if anyone is feeling good, let the person sing a psalm [of praise] (James 5:13).

The schedule of our prayer life should be linked to the weather within. God the Father does not want His children to have unaddressed suffering in their lives. At the heart of ultimate reality is a heart of sympathy. In one of the descriptions of God in the Old Testament, His sympathy is connected to His forgiveness and His graciousness.

> Not **according** to our sins has He dealt with us, and not **according** to our iniquities he has rewarded us.
>
> For **according** to the *height* of the heavens above the earth, His loving loyalty has *overwhelmed* those who deeply respect Him.
>
> **According** to the *distance* from the east to the west, He has *distanced* us from our transgressions.
>
> **According** as a father has deep *compassion* upon his children, Yahweh has deep *compassion* upon those who deeply respect Him (Psalm 103:10-13).

Notice the five "according to's" in the verses. Their use underscores the grace we are under. In complete contrast to what we have done wrong, God has acted as a father toward us and He has completely overwhelmed us with loving loyalty. His conduct toward us has been the direct opposite to our treatment of Him. Verses 11 and 12 use physical dimensions to describe God's grace and forgiveness, and then verse 13 gives the motive driving God's grace—God's compassion.

The New Testament went further than Psalm 103. In the psalm God is like a father. In 2 Corinthians 1:3 He is a Father twice over: a Father to Jesus Christ and a tender Father to us.

> Blessed be the God and Father of our Lord Jesus Christ, the Father of tender mercies and God of every encouragement (2 Corinthians 1:3).

Any healthy father will have as the first thought and question of the day: Are my kids all right? If the offspring are safe, the parents are content. If they are not, the parents want to know and they want to help. God the Father is a better Dad than all the other dads. He wants us to bring our pain and problems to Him.

Weather Reporting

The person who is struggling with temptation, compulsion, and addiction has to recognize the pain in life belongs to God. God's ownership of our pain was purchased by His sympathetic choice to be our Father. As the habit of sharing with God the Father and others grows in the life, the addictive cycle will be stopped in its tracks. Since for the Christian prayer is central in the life of a believer, and since the great prompter for prayer is pain, one would think that Christians should have a natural protection from addiction.

When we do a seminar for couples on skills for marriage, we talk to them about the need for "weather reporting." Weather reporting is simply sharing the happiest moment in the day, the saddest moment in the day, the hurts of the day, and what we would like without demanding it.* Once they have practiced this kind of sharing for awhile, the quality of their relationship seems to improve greatly. We need to do the same with God the Father. He is concerned about what we are going through in life, and we need to share our concerns with Him. As we pray to Him, we obviously pray until we are peaceful.

---

* Our *Healthy Relationships* workbook contains the details of weather reporting. See the end of this book for more information.

The Bible places a great value on having a calm and peaceful emotional life. One of the goals of prayer is to produce that, and one of the aspects of long-term effective prayer is to sustain that. Peter expressed the need this way:

> The completion of everything is at hand, be sensible and sober for prayer (1 Peter 4:7).

Prayer produces serenity and sensibleness, but also serenity and sensibleness can sustain effective prayer. In fact, Jesus taught that thoughtful prayer can keep a person from temptation, the very beginning of the addictive cycle (Matthew 26:41). Of course prayer in the Bible is far more than just dealing with painful emotional states, but that indeed is an important aspect of prayer. Prayer also should be extended to many other areas of life.

Encouraging Your Cravings

Prayer creates not only the backbone to resist addiction, it also creates positive cravings and a deep desire to live continually in the presence of the Trinity. Years ago I experienced the joy of taking my anxieties to God. Over time it became almost automatic. My heart learned not to live with anxiety. Valuing peace, my heart would prompt prayer. But more is involved with prayer than just getting rid of emotional pain. Prayer or fellowship with God should touch every aspect of life.

Jesus and Paul practiced and taught prayer. Jesus taught it straightforwardly oftentimes in direct contradiction to what the religious teachers of His time believed. Paul encouraged prayer and from his written prayers in his letters we can learn much.

Jesus in the Sermon on the Mount had much to say about prayer, and He gave a model prayer. In His comments, He said people ought to pray and not allow the heart to become pained and weak (Luke 18:1). All through the gospels He would teach directly, share stories and parables, and make comments about prayer.

In the gospel of Matthew, He shared a critical order for prayer that revolved around correctly relating to His Father. In the Lord's Prayer He taught His disciples about what healthy prayer would address.* Five different topics appear in order of importance.

1. *The issue of the Father.* Jesus isolated the object of the prayer as the Father in heaven. So the first reality of prayer is that we have a Dad, an Abba-Father in heaven. We are to pray that His name (character, works, and reputation) are significantly set apart in our lives: "Our Father, the One in heaven, let your character, works, and reputation be set apart!" (6:9).

2. *The issue of the Father's will.* After recognizing we have a Father in heaven, we are to recognize that His will is good for us, and we are to ask that it becomes a reality in our lives. Naturally recognizing the value of the first issue, makes the second issue, His will, desirable: "Let Your kingdom come. Let your will become as in heaven also upon earth" (verse 10).

3. *The issue of our needs.* If we are convinced that we have a good Father in heaven whose will is to be desired, we can then more confidently bring all of our needs to Him. The daily bread, a simple need, represents all our needs—physical, emotional, and relational: "Our necessary bread, give to us today" (verse 11).

4. *The issue of forgiveness.* This issue is expressed in such a way that it creates tension. How we forgive others matters to God and should be an issue with us. Notice how numbers 3 and 4 went from our needs to our relationships: "And forgive us our unmet obligations, the way we forgive those who are obligated to us" (verse 12).

---

* The book *Becoming Who God Intended,* chapter 10, pages 218-220, develops more of the context of the Lord's Prayer.

5. *The issue of deliverance from Satan.* This last request recognizes that God is vastly superior to Satan and He is the One who permits the trials that the devil brings: "And you should not bring us into temptation, but rescue us from the evil one" (verse 13).

So the greatest privilege of prayer is a wholesome relationship with the Father in heaven. One can only deal with pain so long. That cannot and should not be the sum and substance of our Christian life. Christianity should go from being a deliverance from wrong and pain to the pleasure of the company of God. Ultimately sinful appetites are replaced with divine affections!

What is noticeable is that our needs and lacks and our painful relationships involving the need for forgiveness comes after acknowledging a Father is in heaven, and His will is our good (we need His will done on earth). As Christians become more and more healthy, the confidence of a Father's care and a happy acceptance of His purposes will precede a preoccupation with needs and soured relationships. The implication of the Lord's Prayer is that we need to deal with who we are before God before we deal with our needs. It is very similar to what we have seen in Colossians 3—identity and relationship precedes pain and appetite.

Prayer then is adjusting our hearts to the heart of God the Father. Our needs and requests are not the essence of prayer. The Father knows what we need before we ask Him (Matthew 6:8). When we conform to who the Father is and how He sees us, we have practiced the essence of prayer. Ultimately it is not our pain or our desires or our needs, it is our good relationship with a Father.

The Great Issues of Conversation with God

I was just at a church near San José, California, presenting a series on Sunday mornings. The members of the class in this fine church were biblically astute and intellectually sharp. Just a great group to teach. We were talking about our identity in Christ and a whole bunch of questions broke out. Then, a woman in the back and on the left side asked a question.

"I understand what you are saying, but I just do not feel loved by God, and I just do not feel like I can trust Him over the years to come. I wonder if He will take his love away if I do not accept it. What can I do about that?" she asked with a look of intensity and concern on her face.

I replied, "May I have your permission to make some observations about your question?" She said yes. When I feel I am going to say something personal about a person in front of a group, I always try to ask for permission.

"In what you just asked, you told me far more about yourself, than you did about God. My guess would be that your experience with life has been one where people have proven to be unreliable, and love has been conditional. So that when you think about God's love, you instinctively assume that won't last too long either."

She stared at me intently, and said, "What can I do about it?"

"One thing that I continually suggest is that you take a walk around the cross in your imagination. Picture yourself walking around the cross observing Christ dying, and keep turning to God the Father and saying to Him that you are grateful that a Son was given for you. Keep thanking Him that you are worth a Son to Him. Keep doing that several times a day for several weeks and watch how your emotions profoundly change."

We talked back and forth some about her anxieties about God's love, and then I asked, "What is your name?" She hesitated, looked embarrassed, and said, "Faith." The whole room burst out laughing, as did I. (She appeared to be good-natured about it, for which I was grateful.)

Making Our Hearts a Comfortable Home

The issues that she raised though are central concerns for prayer. Love and faith are major. They need to be sorted out in prayer. As we adjust our hearts to the Father, certain realities need to be addressed.

We have seen we have an identity in Christ; we have a Father in heaven; we can have a relationship with Him through Christ. But within those realities we don't need to have more information, we need to experience love. Paul the apostle desired intensely that the Ephesian Christians should experience the love of Christ. In the letter to the Ephesian church two prayers were made by the apostle Paul for the church. One prayer is in chapter 1 and the other is in 3. In 3 Paul prayed specifically for certain things to become reality within the lives of the believers. He said he was continually praying to the Father this type of prayer. His prayer was that

> He would grant you, according to the wealth of His glory, to be strengthened with inherent power through His Spirit in the inner person, so that Christ may make a home* in your hearts through faith; that you, being firmly rooted and permanently grounded in love, may be fully able to comprehend with all the saints what is the breadth and length and height and depth, and to experience the love of Christ which surpasses knowledge, that you may be filled up to all the fullness from God (Ephesians 3:16-19).

In his prayer he recognized the presence of the Spirit of God and the necessity that the Spirit of God must apply the truth of God. If this truth was forcefully applied then the believers as a group would have the pleasure of Christ evidencing that He is present in power. The "you" is this passage is plural, meaning "all of you." Paul the apostle is not asking that Christ should come into their lives but He is asking that He might make a home within their lives.

Before we moved into our present home and the previous owners moved out, the house was empty. It was not a home. After we moved in, it had all the evidence of a home: two parents, two kids, and two dogs, plus socks on the bedroom floor left by me. People make a house a home. Faith makes a comfortable home for Christ in the Christians He is already in.

---

* The Greek word for "make a home," often translated as "dwell," refers to truly making a home—as opposed to just being present. Christ indwells us, but we need to make our heart a comfortable home for Him. The church is a house for God (1 Timothy 3:15), but we must by faith make it a home for God (Ephesians 3:16-17).

Paul went from the truth of believers as the home for Christ to further build on that reality. He stated for this home to manifest Christ's life it should be rooted and founded in love. When a house was built in the ancient world, it either was built on rock or holes were dug and filled with rock. A foundation was placed over the rock and the house was built up from the foundation.

For a group of believers to be healthy their lives have to be built on a deep sense of being loved by God the Father. A person who feels loved is a secure person who has a sense of being worthwhile. He or she is delighted in by somebody. Love in the Bible is a delighted passion in another person. In the Old Testament, the word used for God's love when used for people often refers to romantic love, a passionate delight in another person.* A real romance is not informational, and God's love is not informational but sensational. It can be sensed powerfully. Paul said God's love has been poured into the Christian's heart by the Holy Spirit who has been given to us (Romans 5:5). A *pouring* is not a data dump; it is an experience.

As believers have this foundational experience in their lives, they are to exercise faith. Faith exercised will lead to a further experience of being loved by the indwelling Christ, and He will manifest His life in their midst. Others will see that the indwelling Christ is supplying His life to them.

The last result is that the fullness from God the Father will start entering their lives. Those are the results that the Father has to bless His children. God the Father is normally credited within Scripture with producing rich results in the lives of believers.

> Every beneficial thing given and complete gift comes down from the Father of Lights with whom there is no variableness nor shadow of turning (James 1:17).

God has a pattern and plan for the lives of all of His children. Included in this are happy relationships, shared joys, and noble sufferings for Christ and others. He has a life planned for each

---

* See my book *Becoming Who God Intended*, chapter 9, for a detailed development of *agape* love.

of His children so that at the end of it, each will be able to enter heaven with a sense of blessing and accomplishment. This of course can only happen if the believer is planted on a foundation of being deeply delighted in by God, and has exercised faith so that Christ can manifest His life and give an even deeper sense of being loved.

The Issue of Faith

"Let's have a conversation," I said to my acquaintance. He looked happy for the opportunity.

"Here are the rules for a conversation with me," I continued. "Assume that I don't trust you, you are unreliable, and you probably won't follow through."

"Why in heaven's name do you want to talk to me then?" my puzzled if not offended acquaintance said.

"I have to. That's what the culture says I should do. I should have conversations, but I don't feel I should have to trust you or anybody else!"

That little conversation sounds absurd, but those are the kind of conversations God the Father has to live through all day long. With their lips, millions will tell Him how wonderful He is and in their heart they expect nothing from Him.

Faith has to be exercised not only in human relationships but in the divine one with God the Father. Trust is essential for families to work. Trust is essential for the new family. Our faith does not make God trustworthy, but it does open our eyes to see His care especially in the midst of stress and problems.

> Without faith it is impossible to please, for he who is coming to God must believe that He is, and to the ones continually seeking Him that He becomes a wage payer (Hebrews 11:6).

Why does God presume to demand trust? The first reason is that He has given the Divine Son for us. When we think about whether we can trust the Father or not, all He does is point to the dying

Son on the cross. The second is that no relationship can function without faith.

The Issue of Love

So faith is utterly critical in a living relationship or prayer life with the Father. Faith turns loose the Spirit of God to change our lives and the world around us. Faith in prayer also opens to us the vital experience of being delighted in by God. God wants to pour into our lives the unforgettable experience of being loved by God.

> God expressed His depth of love for us in that, as we were doing our sinning, the Son was doing the dying.

Without that experience, Christianity is just a religion. God wants every Christian to have the Jennifer experience. Shortly after her conversion in her late teens, she listened to a sermon and the Spirit of God struck her with impact. She is loved by the divine Father. In all of the vicissitudes of her life, abuse, and betrayal she has had one reality, she is loved by the Father. Storms may wear down Gibraltar, but storms do not move Gibraltar.

> The love from God has been poured out [in the past with a present effect] within our hearts through the Holy Spirit who was given to us (Romans 5:5).

Having a sense of being loved by the Father is the Gibraltar of the Christian life. It should also be an experience sought by the believer in prayer. But such an experience will not occur without trust in the Father's love as expressed in the cross. For God expressed His depth of love for us in that, as we were doing our sinning, the Son was doing the dying.

To make it immensely personal consider the time in your life of your worst sin or greatest humiliation. Picture God the Father meeting you at the time and walking you to the cross so that He can show you what you are worth to Him. We have to combine the personal experiences of our lives with what the Father and Son have done for us. When we place our faith in the Father's love relative to our real sins and our real humiliations, our lives are changed.

Combining faith and love unleashes the power of prayer. Relationships soar on the power of love and trust. Instead of walking into the theme park of addictions, we can choose to associate with our Father in heaven. Instead of living off of the fantasy world, we can live off of our identity in Christ. Instead of the deceptive pleasures of the flesh, the roller coaster of addictions, we can relish the realities of love, joy, and peace. Instead of strained relationships, we can have the freedom of an other-centered heart. Loving those who frustrate us is the greatest of freedoms. The greatest part of all is that we are no longer orphans in an empty world, we are the children of a heavenly Father!

ELEVEN

The Four Life-Changing Experiences

Christianity can handle the worst that the addictive cycle can produce. And Christianity is much more than an antidote to the addictive cycle. It is a set of relationships that are life changing. We have already seen that basic New Testament spirituality can take the addiction cycle apart. But behind that basic spirituality are four life-changing experiences. Spirituality is a process, but those life-changing experiences form the spinal column of the process. To have these experiences is to have the skeleton necessary to flesh out the process of spirituality and addiction-proofing. We will see what those life-changing experiences are, how they relate to Christian spirituality, and how they take the addictive cycle apart by looking at the incredible life of Tammy Jo Wickersheim.

Tammy Jo was born in a chaotic home after her mom was sexually involved with a former husband. At five years of age Tammy was raped by an older brother and left bleeding in a barn. Along with him, other stepbrothers would abuse her. When she hid in closets, under the porch, or the house, they would stalk her, find her, and abuse her.

To end the torment she started running away when she was 12. Her stepfather and her mom were in the pornography business at the time. Safety for Tammy was in living on the streets and not in the home. That was where she often went. When she was home, the abuses surrounding that business found her.

At 14 her Chinese stepfather, one of a number of stepdads, gave her away in a marriage to an abusive young man. She had a baby, and after that she ran away from the husband and took her baby with her. He would find her and steal the baby and force her to return to be with the baby. During all this time she was a self-proclaimed atheist. (Not an unreasonable belief for a terribly abused person.)

At 19 she went to a church for the first time in her life. Having been verbally coerced to go, she showed up in a miniskirt and flamboyant clothes. To her shock and absolute delight, she heard the gospel, believed it, and met God. Tammy got radically saved. That is pretty much normal for someone from her background. She just fell in love with Jesus. She felt she had a new spirit and was a genuinely different person.

She discovered that who she was, was more important to God than what she had done or what was done to her. This gave her permission to not hide but to associate.

The First Great Experience: A New Identity

She also began to see herself in a profoundly different way. She started the process of seeing herself the way God the Father saw her. She walked into the church building believing she was a product of evolution, with no more significance than a bug she could crush with her hand. When she was a teenager that is how she explained life to one of her brothers: There is no God, and bugs and people are equal and die the same death.

She walked into the church having no worth, instinctively believing she had no more value than the trash in the garbage can outside. She walked in not necessarily with a burden of guilt—but at the core of her being shame boiled and festered.

In the church she started down the pathway of seeing herself in a profoundly different way. She found out that God thought she was worth dying for. She heard that God recognized the horror and the violence and the wrong that was in the world. Indeed God was determined to rescue the people of the world through His Son. She heard that God loved her. In a very short time, a mere 45 minutes, she was presented with an incredibly different way of seeing herself, and she believed it. She believed it so deeply (and the Spirit so enveloped her) that she had the experience that would alter the rest of her life. At that point she was given a different vision of herself that would stubbornly cling to her through the host of gut-wrenching experiences awaiting her.

Lack of Affirmation

After the church service and her profession of faith, a roaring fire of change came into her life. This fire, though, was not fanned by those who led her to Christ.

Having been victimized all of her life, Tammy now fell under a different form of abuse: the neglect that many churches practice. No one found her to disciple her. She was left the way the great majority of new believers are left, without nurture. She had an experience but no one gave her a framework for those experiences. No one taught her how to live for God.

What should have been done was first to find her and then to disciple her. The disciplers should have built on this sense of being a new person in a new world by teaching her that God saw her in a profoundly different way than she saw herself. She already sensed that she was made in the image of God, and that she was not the product of evolution. Her newfound view of herself should have been aggressively augmented. She should have been told that she was now clothed in Christ. She was not the sum total of what had been done to her in the past, but she was now the sum total of what Christ had done for her in the present.

> You are all mature sons and daughters of God through faith in Christ Jesus. For all of you who were immersed into Christ have clothed yourselves with Christ (Galatians 3:26-27).

If they had taken time, they should have told her just as she had a family history from her past, God has a new family history for her now. God the Father shares His Son's history with every one who becomes His child through faith. From His perspective she too suffered with Christ for her wrongdoing. She too died with Him on the cross. She was buried also in the limestone tomb. She also came out of the grave with Him to a living relationship with God. From His perspective she is now part of a new creation.

If someone had taught her these basic truths of Christianity when she was a new convert, she could have built easily on the wonderful experience she had in conversion. Instead of eventually being trapped by her past, she could have found a totally different way of seeing herself. The new habit of seeing herself as God sees her that started with her conversion could have become the foundation of her Christian life.

But sadly, she had to wait years, until a few godly women from New Seasons Church in Portland, Oregon, began to disciple her and pour their lives into hers. She would then learn that her whole relationship with God was based on her union with Christ, and that union (or new way of seeing herself) should become one of those four critical experiences.

> Knowing this by experience, that our old identity was crucified with Him, in order that our body of sin might be nullified, so that we would no longer be slaves to sin (Romans 6:6).

Fully embracing God's new way of seeing ourselves, and experiencing the fact that our old identity or way of seeing ourselves was crucified (killed) would result in no longer being enslaved to the sinful habits of the past.

With this new identity she would have had the ability to deal with the fantasy world that sustains addiction. She was struggling with three addictions but at the time she did not have names for two of them: One was codependency, the second was a form of food addiction, anorexia, and the last was smoking. She threw herself into consuming relationships with men while living off of the emotional highs that provided, and at the same time she fixated on the negative aspects of her body. If she had had a clear picture of who she was in Christ, recovery would have been quicker.

The Second Great Experience: Being Valued as a Person

Also in her conversion another of the great experiences blossomed in Tammy's heart: the sense of being valued. Who she was as a person was more important to God than what she had done. As she listened to the gospel in that church, she heard that God through His Son Jesus had died for everything that she had done wrong, her sins. With that came the irresistible idea that she mattered to God.

There is nothing more overwhelming to experience than who we are is vastly more important to God than what we have done.

> We ourselves were once foolish, unbelieving, going wrong, being continually *enslaved to appetites* and many different pleasures, being led by evil and envy, hateful, while hating each other. But when the kindliness of God our Savior and affection for humanity appeared, *not on the basis of deeds which we have done in righteousness,* but according to His mercy, He saved us by the washing of regeneration and renewing by the Holy Spirit, whom He poured out upon us richly through Jesus Christ our Savior, so that being justified by His grace we would be made heirs according to the hope of eternal life (Titus 3:3-7).

Not on the basis of deeds we have done in righteousness, but on the basis of who we are to Him and His compassion for our person is why the Lord saved us. Christianity becomes a divine romance when the heart grasps this truth. It is not what we have done right or wrong; it is who we are that matters to God.

Grasping this truth and integrating it into our hearts has a massive effect on the addictive cycle. When the heart feels this truth, it can come with its struggles and failures to God the Father. Transparency replaces shameful hiding. The struggling and addicted Christian can much more freely come to God if he or she thinks that God values who they are more than what they have done right or wrong.

Getting the Cart Before the Horse

But that did not happen. Tammy was not discipled. She was allowed to drift. Since she loved Jesus, her own sincerity set her up for disaster. She heard from the bits and pieces of information that flow through a church that Christians should not smoke and should not get divorced.

Of course she quit smoking and out of naïve obedience went back to her non-Christian husband to save the doomed marriage. His abuse continued; his affairs continued; his witchcraft continued. A daughter was born to the couple. In the midst of all of that Tammy was anorexic and was down to 97 pounds. Thinking she was fat, she was preoccupied with her weight. Furthermore, the marriage was gasping for life. The marriage ended with the husband stealing the son so he would not be exposed to Christianity and he disappeared.

Afterward she came across Teen Challenge ministries to street girls, and she threw herself into that. Displaying again the fanaticism and the gifting the Lord gave her, she became a chaplain, counselor, and teacher for street girls. She and her daughter lived together at Teen Challenge. When her daughter was four years of age, the little girl fell from the monkey bars and broke her arm. The trauma from the fall caused her to have a heart attack. After eight days, she was taken off of life support. Another disaster was added to the many Tammy's life had absorbed. From the pain of that experience, she fled to England to try and find her son.

The pain was wider and deeper than the Atlantic Ocean she had flown across. She wanted to have a quickly spreading cancer or a nasty accident so she could go to be with God. Instead God came to her.

She looked for her former husband and her son Carlos in England and did not find them. In Birmingham she was walking in the city and she wandered into an overgrown English garden with a high stone wall around it. She sat down in the garden and began to worship God in the midst of her pain. As she was sitting there, she began to hear a song in her heart. She had never heard the words before. She listened and she heard:

> *I have called you to serve me gloriously,*
> *I have chosen you to be my own.*
> *I have called you to me gloriously*
> *Someday you'll dance before my throne.*

Over and over again the song soared through her heart. The fog of pain and darkness was still there but a sun was rising through with the sound of the words. She started to sing responsively from her own heart with the same words. The love within those words, the promise of those words, and the faithfulness of those words all were inundating her.

Tammy felt that those words gave her a sense of having a future under the care of God. In the garden she danced. She was loved. The music of heaven assured her of that. She fled from her pain and God met her in her pain. And when He met her in her pain, He met her with a song of love.

The Third Great Experience: Being Loved

The inheritance of every believer is to have an individual experience of being loved. For the individual believer and a church of believers that is one of the four foundational experiences of Christianity. That sense of being loved breaks through the incredible isolation that people such as Tammy have experienced in life.

Paul the apostle assumed that every believer should have that experience. A normative Christianity exists and Paul gave one of the key elements.

> This hope [of character development] is not shaming, because the delighted passion [*agape* love] of God has been poured out within our hearts through the Holy Spirit who was given to us (Romans 5:5).

The word "poured" in the verse implies that this is an experience that Paul is describing and not a deposit of information. Many evangelicals assume that *agape* love is an act of the will but "acts of the will" are not poured into people's hearts, feelings are.

Sadly, many who call themselves Christians, and also Christians themselves, do not have this experience because they instinctively view Christianity as a barter system: We exchange our obedience for His love and blessing. That is false. The kind of love that is poured out is pictured in the next verse (Romans 5:6). The verse says that God the Father recommends His *agape* love towards us in that while we were continually sinners Christ died for us. The beauty of this love is that it is not based on what we have done right or wrong but it is based on God's affection for us.

That is the defining picture of Christianity. God the Son is on the cross suffering for our sins, and the Father is looking at us and is saying, "We love you more than we are disgusted by your sin. Who you are is precious to us. You are loved and delighted in. You are worth dying for."

Being Rooted and Grounded

This experience of being individually loved is also critical for the healthy life of a church. In Ephesians 3, Paul the apostle prayed that the Christians in Ephesus should have a personal experience of being loved:

> ...that He would grant all of you, according to the riches of His glory, to be strengthened with power through His Spirit in the inner person, so that Christ may make a home in your hearts through faith; that all of you, *having been rooted and grounded in love,* may be able to comprehend with all the saints what is the breadth and length and height and depth, and *to experience the love of Christ* which surpasses knowledge, that all of you may be filled up to all the fullness from God (Ephesians 3:16-19).

Christians should become a comfortable home for Christ where He can manifest His life among the believers. This can only happen if the believers are grounded and founded on a deep experience of being loved. As they exercise faith on this foundational experience, they further experience the personal love of Christ for them.

This experience of being loved is normative for every believer, but again because of barter-system Christianity, few believers seem to have a sense of being deeply liked by God. It is not unusual for God the Father to hunt down deeply hurting Christians like Tammy to personally invade their lives so they can have this precious experience.

Again being loved is one of those four fundamental experiences. Such a profound sensation encourages the person to associate with God the Father as opposed to disassociate and stepping into the fantasy world. This powerful and strong experience gives permission to the Christian to confidently come to the Father with the struggles of addiction.

Love touches the depths of the human person deeper than any addiction. Guilt, shame, and worthlessness may taint the soul but God's delighted passion will penetrate further. The value of being loved is that it draws out our love and leads us to pursue God the Father. First John 1:19 says that we love because He first loved us. Love has no greater experience than that.

When Tammy was in the garden, the Lord invaded the pain in

her heart with His presence. In a very real sense, He invaded the addictive cycle at the beginning by meeting the pain head-on. The experience taught Tammy that God was not afraid of her pain. His love could go deeper than her pain. The first two elements of the addictive cycle were addressed, pain and disassociation.

Tammy failed in her attempt to find her son, Carlos, but God succeeded in finding her with His love. That experience was emblazoned on her heart. Since she could not find him, she returned to the States. For two months she sat by her daughter's grave in Vacaville, California. A total stranger came into her life who told her he was a Wycliffe missionary and it was God's will for them to marry. They did and within a week he was abusing Tammy. The missionary story was a lie, but he said instead God had sent him on a mission to break her spirit. He said that he heard voices and the voice was that of God's. Shortly after the marriage she had a beautiful baby girl. The marriage fell apart and the court awarded her full custody of the child.

The court placed her and her child under its protection and placed a restraining order on the man. He started stalking her and she went into hiding. Where she stayed she made a bed for her daughter in a bathtub, and she slept in the bathroom with a loaded gun and a butcher knife.

She fled to Sacramento, California. A church-going ex–Green Beret volunteered to protect her. After a time she became involved with him. She thought she was safe because he was an usher in the church and was well-liked. But he had two major secrets: He was a closet alcoholic, and he had six previous wives!

Moving Toward Freedom

The couple moved to the Pacific Northwest, and that relationship fell apart. Along the way Tammy had picked up medical training, and she worked in a medical clinic. Amazingly she continued in her ministry to teenagers and the down and out. She had no sense of how to set limits on her life, and she wanted to do things for her Savior.

During the days she was the charge nurse for a busy urgent care clinic. In the nights she threw herself into a church planting team. In her church life she led a women's ministry and the youth group. Finally she had a breakdown and could not function. For nine months she was too weak to walk or to care for herself and her daughter.

A perceptive pastor and his wife came into Tammy's life at that time, and they asked her if she had been abused. With that question the river of sorrow, hurt, and shame poured out of her. For the first time in her life she told someone else what had been done to her. They listened and loved her. They prayed with her over the tragedies of her life. She felt those experiences losing their sting and torment as she shared with others. She was becoming free of their stranglehold.

The Fourth Great Experience: An Abba Father

As I was reading the notes that Tammy had given me, I noticed that she put the experience of dealing with the anorexia that had haunted her entire life with the experience of discovering that she had a Father in heaven. But she had not explained how one was related to the other. So I called her and said that in her notes the two things were joined but there was no explanation as to how they were related.

She explained that after becoming a Christian she had hated the thought that God was a Father. She liked Jesus. She loved to talk to Him, but she felt like vomiting over the thought that God could be a Father. But she went through material in her early 20s that taught God was a Father. In fact, the teaching said, He was the best of Fathers. She learned that information but it still did not sink in until the Spirit of God nudged her. She was driving along singing to herself about being a servant of Jesus and the Spirit impressed her that she should be singing about being a daughter of God. So she changed the song and her heart was changed in the process.

As she thought through the insight that God was indeed her real "Dad," she had to come to terms with her illegitimate birth. She was told and always felt that she was a mistake. It seemed to play out in the self-rejection and the body hatred that surfaced with anorexia. She could always find something to despise about her body. She felt fat even when her ribs were sticking out so much they could easily be counted.

But if God was her Father and He had created her, then she could not be a mistake. She could not be imperfect. She could relax with who she is. The dread hold of anorexia began to loosen. *She* was not her weight; *she* was not her fat. She was a well-loved daughter of God. She was the offspring that God wanted. She felt the significance of the words of the psalmist.

> You yourself formed my kidneys (the depths of me); You wove me in my mother's womb. I will give thanks to You, for I am awesomely and miraculously made; Miraculous are Your works, And my soul knows it very well (Psalm 139:13-14).

Those words and others like them helped Tammy to understand that she was not a mistake. A Father in heaven wanted her and formed her. Every believer should have the experience of sensing that he or she has an affectionate Dad in heaven. It is one of the basic experiences of Christianity. That has huge implications not as information but as an integrated reality. It means we are not alone. One of the major ministries of the Spirit to the believer is to get that message across.

> Because all of you are adult sons, God sent the Spirit of His adult Son into our hearts, continually shouting, "Abba Father!" (Galatians 4:6).

The significance of that for the addictive cycle is that it attacks the disassociation that is necessary for the cycle. We are reminded that we are not abandoned. Jesus at the worst moment in His earthly life while He was in the Garden of Gethsemane turned to God and prayed, "Abba, Father" or Daddy Father (Mark 14:36). As we grow in our spiritual life, as we learn from the Spirit, He shouts at us about our Abba Father. As we grow in maturity we learn to shout back.

> You have not received a spirit of slavery leading to fear again, but you have received a spirit of adoption as mature sons by which we continually shout, "Abba! Father!" (Romans 8:15).

As we experience God as a Father we are being freed to grow. This experience gives us the incentive to pray for we recognize that we matter to Him. It addresses the profound aloneness that many from unhealthy family backgrounds experience. It addresses the pain, for the Father is there to comfort us in our pain (2 Corinthians 1:3-5). We have a relationship in which we are valued and loved.

A number of the elements of the addictive cycle are addressed by the experience of an Abba Father. Pain, disassociation, the fantasy world all are significantly addressed. Every time a Christian realistically turns to the Father in prayer the tentacles of the addictive cycle are weakened, and the superhighway of spirituality is widened.

The Good Dad

Tammy was crossing the great divide between addiction and grace and she was entering the healthy lands. She connected with a Christian counselor, and she started seeing the patterns that had made for so much misery in her life. As she pursued health, she also pursued a deepening relationship with her Abba Father. For any great exploration of the past should be made in the company of a good Dad. For the first time in 12 years, she cried, and then she cried and cried. She came to terms with her dependency. She no longer needed to have men in her life. In previous times when she did not have a man in her life, she succumbed to panic attacks. The panic attacks subsided; she could be by herself.

She then went to Multnomah School of the Bible to learn more about her Father God, the Son her Savior, and the ministry of the Holy Spirit. While there she met a music minister of New Seasons Church, Bruce Wickersheim, who had never been married. Then, this most unlikeliest of couples married. In the midst of her life, she finally met a reliable man who loved her. She married and she continued to put her soul together.

I met them because I was preaching at Good Shepherd Church in Oregon. Bruce is the music director and he laughed at all my jokes and even laughed at the material that I did not think was a joke. We shared what the Lord was doing in our lives, and as I listened to Tammy Wickersheim, I thought her life experience dramatically illustrated the power of those four experiences.

The Four Experiences: The Foundation for Growth

Addiction is an experience. A great set of experiences is needed to drive that experience out. We Christians believe in the Trinity, but the great need is to live in the presence of the Trinity. The difference is between being a child in the jungles of Brazil and looking at pictures of snow fall as opposed to being in a real snowstorm. We need to travel from knowing biblical information to experiencing and integrating truth.

> For the individual, these four experiences are the absolute bedrock foundation of mental and relational health.

As the gospel contains basic information about what needs to be believed in order to be saved, the New Testament in the writings of Paul has a basic set of four experiences every believer should have. They are essentially simple experiences very much similar to what a well-loved child would experience in a healthy home. In a healthy home, the child would experience

1. a caring, affectionate dad.

2. a sense of being loved.

3. being valued—that who he or she is more important than what wrong or right things the child may have done.

4. that the parents have a different perspective on him or her than what the child him or herself has. The young child may be frustrated by not being able to read and feels like a failure while the parents see the child as reading in a year or two. This positive identity with the parents becomes a source of deep and growing confidence.

For the individual, these four experiences are the absolute bedrock foundation of mental and relational health. In therapy those are often as not missing in the lives of those who are being helped.

The four basic spiritual experiences are

1. a sense of having a Father in heaven.

2. a sense of being loved by the Father.

3. a sense of being valued for who I am versus what I have done.

4. a sense of being seen differently by the Father than how I may initially see myself.

These experiences are obviously interrelated. But they involve the foundational realities: the Fatherhood of God, the love of God, the nature of the atonement, and our union with Christ. If you look at chart 1 on the following page, you will see how these four great experiences challenge the addictive cycle.

Two more parts of the addictive cycle exist, those of the initial act and acting out, but those are the least important parts of the cycle. If pain, disassociation, and the fantasy world are dealt with, the remaining two are essentially powerless.

The four experiences actually make up the background of Christian spirituality according to Paul, as we have seen in Colossians 3. In chapter 3 the pattern of Paul and the experiences connect as shown in chart 2 on the next page.

Chart 1

The Addictive Cycle	The Four Experiences
Pain	**Love:** The love of the Father goes deeper than pain and draws the heart toward God the Father.
Disassociation	**Abba Father:** The reality of having a Father in heaven draws the addict out of disassociation and into the best of associations. **Being valued:** This frees the heart from crippling guilt and shame and encourages the person to come to God for help.
Fantasy world	**Being seen differently:** This is a direct assault on the fantasy world, for it frees the imagination to its proper use. The proper use is to see the world and ourselves in the eyes of God.

Chart 2

Paul's Pattern in Colossians 3	The Four Experiences
New identity in Christ (verses 1-2)	1. Being seen differently by God the Father
Seeking the heavenly relationships (verses 1-2)	4. Sensing God as an Abba Father
Putting to death moods and lusts (verse 5)	2. Sensing being valued 3. Sensing being loved
Taking off relational pain (verses 8-9)	2. Sensing being valued 3. Sensing being loved
Putting on sympathy (verse 12)	2. Sensing being valued 3. Sensing being loved

The greatest growth occurs in the Christian life when we allow God to address our greatest weaknesses. Some of those weaknesses are evident such as pornography addiction or binging and purging, others are not because they are the long established habits of spiritual flabbiness. As those spiritual weaknesses are transformed, deep growth becomes possible, affection for God and others blossoms, and mature other-centered Christianity results.

Tammy has experienced the power of those experiences. Their greatest value is of course the relational. As we step out of temptation, compulsion, and addiction we discover we are in the presence of great company, the Trinity. We discover character we thought we never had. We are introduced to ourselves by God to discover who we truly are in the eyes of God.

A World of Walking Forward into Relationships

We have journeyed through the world of temptation, compulsion, and addiction, as well as the world as God created it. In the journey we have seen that addiction is really a lonely life without relationships. Addiction also chooses the good things of life over God and relationships. Addiction is the World of walking backward, where a person walks away from other people and from God.

We have seen that dealing with temptation, compulsion, and addiction in the areas of food and sexual addiction is not a simple process of doing the right thing. The depths of the human heart are involved, and the grace of God is desperately needed. The great problem of addiction and temptation is that it can create a repeated cycle of defeat in the lives of people.

Christian Spirituality and the Addictive Cycle

Temptation, compulsion, and addiction create a cycle that a person repeats over and over again. It starts with pain (sometimes physical and sometimes emotional) and stress. The human heart hates pain, as it should, but instead of sorting out the pain relationally or through medical help, the person plunges after a pleasure that will drown the pain.

The pain can be as simple as loneliness or as nasty as repeated beatings. In an automatic response the person steps into non-relationship, or disassociation. Sliding from that to the fantasy world that sustains whatever the addictive behavior may be, the person initiates a robot-like activity. The result can be overeating or it can be repeatedly visiting a pornographic site. Eventually if nothing intervenes, significant damage will enter the person's life.

Normal Christian spirituality is able to take the addictive cycle apart. A common difficulty though is that in the Christian culture information has been substituted for integration. So we have to be sure that the spirituality we are speaking of results in true integration with the changing of instincts. Obviously addiction is entirely instinctive: thought ruins it! So the Christian spirituality has to be one of the instincts.

The New Testament has a pattern of spirituality challenging every aspect of the cycle. Colossians 3 gives the elements challenging the cycle. Christian spirituality starts with our identity in Christ. That addresses the most dangerous element in the addictive cycle, the fantasy world. On the basis of our union with Christ, we can associate with God the Father and deal with areas of pain, discomfort, and desire. As we go through this process we can develop deep sympathy for others and instead of disassociating we can actually become other-centered like Christ.

The great loss in addiction is relationships, and the great gain in spirituality is the deep companionship of others.

The Great Experiences Become Our New Instincts

Christian spirituality is built upon the four great experiences we discussed in the previous chapter. These are having a sense of an Abba Father in heaven, feeling this Father's love and affection, recognizing we are more valued for whom we are rather than what we have done, and finally recognizing we are seen differently by the Father than how we see ourselves. I lately received an e-mail from a young Christian woman working with Campus Crusade in Boise, Idaho. Her words beautifully illustrate the power of instincts based on the great experiences, in contrast to the mere possession of information.

> I am writing to you today because I have good news. A lost part of my heart has been found. I think it will make sense if I give you some background information. For the last few months, I have been reading your book *Becoming Who God Intended*. I have to say that I have really been enjoying it. I have gained more insight and understanding to how the Lord changes past pictures to healthy ones in order to heal the heart.
>
> Yesterday, I was spending the day with a close friend who has four-month-old twins. I love those twins, and they are so precious to me; I would die for them. As I was alone I was reflecting: Those babies don't have to do anything, and they are loved. Actually, they can be frustrating with all their cries, demands, required cleaning, and constant care, but I still can't resist loving and wanting the best for them. They also just soak up all the love and smile back at me! I thought, *They are not even my own children, and I love them so much. How much more will I love my own children when I do have them?*
>
> And then, like lightning it hit me: I *am* a child of the Father, and He loves me even more perfectly and passionately as His daughter than I could ever love a child of mine. Dr. Eckman, *He loves me!* The heavenly Father loves me! He not only loves me, but He sees me as worthy to be part of His great plan! I have known that for 26 years, but now I *feel* it deep down in my inmost being. I have experienced it in my heart. You are right when you say, "Emotions do not authenticate the truth, but emotions do authenticate our *understanding and integration* of the truth." I cried for joy for hours as I felt the Father's love just penetrate, soften, and heal my heart so I could experience His love and passionate delight for me.

The exciting news is, this is just the beginning. God is not done yet. If the reality of His love feels so good now, how much more will it be so when the Lord is finished healing my heart completely and even when I see Him face to face? My released heart just wants to declare the miracle of His love to the world...and that if He could do this in my heart, it can happen for anyone.

This young woman is describing two of the great experiences: The first is having a Father in heaven, and the second is a sense of being delighted in by Him. She said that for 26 years she knew the information, but now she *feels* the information. *Feeling* these truths creates the necessary backbone for unleashing Christian spirituality to take apart the addictive cycle. These experiences give power to the process of Colossians 3 so that spirituality is not a technique but a relationship.

We have seen this truth blossoming in life after life. Christian spirituality properly lived is the summons of death for the addictive cycle. With the gospel of Christ comes an other-centered life liberating us from the blackmail of the fantasy world and the power of the flesh.

Our goal is to seek the Father through Christ. His goal is our liberation. And beyond the wonderful benefit of liberation from addiction, compulsion, and temptation is the very best benefit: Our liberation to live in a world of growing, fruitful relationships with the Trinity and with other people.

BECOMING WHAT GOD INTENDED MINISTRIES
An Invitation to Experience God's Loyal Love

BWGI Ministries is a nonprofit organization dedicated to proclaiming God the Father's loyal love, the efficacy of Christ's work, and the power of the believer's identification with Him.

We offer the following resources:

- worldwide Christian leadership training

- seminars

- community outreaches

- small-group resources

- our new e-learning courses

A Personal Invitation

David Eckman invites you to join him online for a sample session on worth and identity based on a careful look at Romans chapters 5 and 6. *This is free for you.* Through video, audio, PowerPoint, and creative and accurate translations of the Bible, let him show you the wonderful truths about your worth and identity—truths that are actually in the Bible! Go to **www.bwgi.org/more** for this session.

How to Contact BWGI Ministries

Web site:	**www.WhatGodIntended.com**
Address:	BWGI Ministries
	3037 Hopyard Road, Suite P
	Pleasanton, CA 94588
Telephone:	**(925) 846-6264**
E-mail:	webmail@bwgi.org

Seminars

BWGI Ministries offers a total of 5 seminars. Each one has a lasting impact on individuals and transforms their relationship with God.

We have a team of talented and experienced presenters that will make any seminar an event to remember. Please visit our Web site at **www.BWGI.org** or call us at **925-846-6264** for more information on seminar bookings for your church or organization.

- ## Setting the Heart Free
  This seminar focuses on freeing the heart from guilt and worthlessness so a believer can experience an adult relationship with God, which is not based on performance. This results in an ability to live the Christian life with lasting gratitude.

- ## Healthy Relationships
  Healthy relationships flow out of healthy identities, compassionate listening, and other-centeredness. The seminar teaches attendees how to acquire such abilities, and what it means to be made in the image of God. It goes on to address what it means to be male and female.

- ## Addiction-Proofing Your Life and Family
  Discover how a healthy spirituality directly challenges addiction. This seminar addresses four of the most common addictions that cause individuals and ministries to fall: food, sex, alcohol, and gambling. Identifying gender differences in regards to addictions, it equips participants with biblical principles that have proven effective for breaking addiction.

- ## Healthy Leadership
  This seminar presents biblically based principles of leadership for the leader, the team, and the congregation. Everything flows out of our identity in Christ. It goes beyond sterile principles to show how the leader can influence others through relationships, goal-setting, and creating a healthy leadership environment.

- ## Creating a Healthy Family
  This seminar is an excellent outreach event, partnering BWGI Ministries and sponsoring churches within a community. The event consists of a three-hour community lecture on family relationships, followed by seven weeks of small-group meetings. The small groups are formed from interested participants after the lecture. (Typically, more than a third of those who attend the lecture choose to join a small group.)

Products and Resources

BWGI Ministries produces books, audiotape sets, pamphlets, and video materials designed to help you grow and mature spiritually in Christ. Our materials have been proven over many years, and we are confident about their effectiveness in restoring the dynamic personal relationship with Christ that God the Father intends for all believers.

Books by David Eckman

- Becoming What God Intended: A Study for Spiritual Transformation
  This life-changing 186-page workbook is designed to help the Christian achieve an emotionally rich spiritual life in the presence of God. **Price: $18.00**

- Becoming What God Intended: A Study for Spiritual Transformation, Facilitator's Guide
  This Facilitator's Guide will assist you in leading a small group through a 12-week program using the workbook above. **Price: $20.00**

- Creating a Healthy Family: Breaking the Dysfunctional Cycle
  This 165-page, 6-week workbook, the first in a series, gives a strategy for both short-term and long-term change. It explains the effects of a stressful family background on an adult, and how that can be positively changed. **Price: $12.00**

- Healthy Relationships for Singles & Couples
  This book is designed to naturally follow *Creating a Healthy Family*. It addresses how individuals should function in relationships. The goal of this book is to teach how to become an interdependent team. **Price: $12.00**

Audiotapes and CDs by David Eckman

- Becoming What God Intended: A Study for Spiritual Transformation
  This series of 12 talks forms the background for the *Becoming What God Intended* workbook, acting as a Christian life conference for those who are ready for God to be the change agent for their inner lives. **Price: $35.00**

- Setting the Heart Free
  This set of six talks is a study in the book of Romans that isolates the three core values that change human personality: a guilt-free environment, a worthwhile relationship with God as Father, and a new identity in Christ. **Price: $22.00**

- From Tears to Diamonds
  This series of four talks describes how a person can deal with the great tragedies of life, explaining not only how to understand such tragedies, but also how to find benefit from them. **Price: $22.00**

- Life After Death: Learn How to Rid Your Heart of the Fear of Death

  Gain the confidence every person needs when thinking about death. The victory of Christ is not just over sin, the devil, the world, and guilt—it is also a victory over death. In this talk, Dr. Eckman looks at several passages of Scripture to see how Christ has conquered death and how we have victory over death through Him. God's intention is that the great enemy of humanity, death, should not blackmail you! **Price: $7.00**

- Knowing God's Heart: Learn How God Views You— It's Better Than You Think!

  All of us carry around a picture of ourselves painted across our hearts that is the foundation for all of our relationships. God's picture of the Christian is deeply connected to His Son. Through faith, we have been joined to Christ, and that union is the basis of a truly healthy relationship with God. **Price: $7.00**

- Identity in Christ: Learn How to Rid Your Heart of Guilt and Shame

  The discovery that God is not preoccupied with your sin sets the stage for realizing the power of the love of God to be experienced and expressed in your life. Discover how the ancient descriptions of the tabernacle in Exodus and Leviticus reinforce the truth of where God's heart is. As you listen, allow these truths of the gospel of Jesus Christ to wash over you and transform your relationship to Jesus to one of deep appreciation, acceptance, and love. **Price: $7.00**

Videotape by David Eckman

- Creating a Healthy Family: Breaking the Dysfunctional Cycle

  This four-part video lecture (two videotapes) gives a strategy for both short-term and long-term change, explaining the effects of a stressful family background on an adult, and how that can be positively changed. The video addresses the emotional scars underlying compulsive behavior, confusion, and diminished self-worth, offering solutions that are immediately applicable. The tapes are broken into four sections to facilitate use with small groups. Use the workbook in conjunction with this video series for best impact. **Price: $39.00**

E-Learning

Based on the seminars and courses taught for many years, BWGI Ministries will be offering unique e-learning ("distance learning") courses from our Web site, **www.BWGI.org**. A number of different levels will be available, depending on your situation, budget, and available time. The courses will also be available for credit from several institutions of higher learning.

BWGI Ministries' e-learning courses begin with the materials similar to a typical distance-learning course. But that is where the similarities end. BWGI Ministries' courses include access to and interaction with a course mentor. The course mentor is very familiar with the course material—typically having taught it or assisted with the teaching process at seminars and in classrooms. The student communicates with the mentor in several ways: via an online password-protected forum, a private messenger system, and by telephone.

The mentor is available for answering questions and giving assistance in areas of confusion and difficulty. In addition, the mentor will ask questions of the student to gauge progress and understanding level. Quizzes and papers will be expected from the student, and feedback from the mentor will be provided on submitted homework. In the case of a student seeking course credit, a grade will be assigned at the end of the course. The first course being offered is—

• Spiritual Life Development

2 semester hours work

This profoundly biblical course is designed to integrate the core values of Christianity into a person's instincts as well as create an emotionally rich environment within, resulting in a truly outward-focused person. This will occur within lectures that are richly Bible-based. It can be taken for credit or non-credit on the graduate level.

"I strongly urge you to get Becoming Who God Intended *and put it to work in your life."*

—Josh McDowell

Becoming Who God Intended

David Eckman

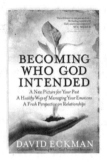

Whether you realize it or not, your imagination is filled with *pictures* of reality. The Bible indicates these pictures reveal your true "heart beliefs"—the beliefs that actually shape your everyday feelings and reactions to family, friends, and others, to life's circumstances, and to God.

Perhaps you're...

- struggling with anxiety, guilt, or habitual sins
- frustrated because your experience doesn't seem to match what the Bible talks about
- wondering if your emotions and feelings fit into the Christian life at all

David Eckman compassionately shows you how to allow God's Spirit to build new, *biblical* pictures in your heart and imagination. As you do this, you will be able to accept God's acceptance of you in Christ, break free of negative emotions and habitual sins...and finally experience the life God the Father has always intended for you.

"David Eckman is a man you can trust...
His teaching resonates with God's wisdom and compassion."

—**Stu Weber,** author of *Tender Warrior* and
Four Pillars of a Man's Heart